*FALSE
PRESENCE
OF THE
KINGDOM*

The Technological Society
Propaganda
The Political Illusion
A Critique of the New Commonplaces
The Presence of the Kingdom
The Theological Foundation of Law
Violence
To Will and to Do
The Meaning of the City
Prayer and Modern Man

FALSE
PRESENCE
OF THE
KINGDOM

Jacques Ellul

Translated by
C. Edward Hopkin

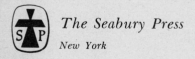 *The Seabury Press*
New York

First published in France in the series, *"Les Bergers et les Mages,"* 1963.

Copyright © 1972 by The Seabury Press, Incorporated
Library of Congress Catalog Card Number: 77-163969
736-272-C-6
Design by Paula Wiener

Printed in the United States of America

Preface

This essay is obviously related to my other writings. It is based upon them to the extent that hurried assertions, or topics merely mentioned in passing, are developed extensively elsewhere. I take the liberty of referring the reader to the following works:

The Theological Foundation of Law
The Presence of the Kingdom
L'Homme et l'Argent
Propaganda: The Formation of Men's Attitudes
"Nation et Nationalisme," *Revue de l'Evangélisation,* 1960
"Mythes Modernes," *Diogène,* 1958
"Signification actuelle de la Réforme," *Foi et Vie,* 1959
"Désacralisation et Resacralisation dans le Monde Moderne," *Semeur,* 1963.

Furthermore, many political evaluations relate to a

larger work with the title: *The Political Illusion*. In particular, one will find there discussion of the term "political"; politics and values; the current situation; the influence of news reports; autonomy versus politics; the centers of political decision, etc.

J.E.

TO THE AMERICAN READER

While I am describing and discussing in the text situations and policy decisions of the Reformed Church in France, these situations and policy decisions are not peculiar to the experience of French Christians. Their experience has now been duplicated in most other churches. Theological debate in the French Church on the role of the Christian in society is often far advanced over such debate in other countries; this may be explained by the fact that the French have lived for a longer time under a secularized society, where the situation of the Church is a much weaker one. But such debate is important for everyone, and for what will happen in the next few years. The American reader will, therefore, be able in almost every instance to find for himself the appropriate parallel situation in the American Church. Indeed, because he is examining the experience in the French Church, he may even better understand my evaluations and theological criticisms.

Contents

Preface   v

Introduction   1

PART I: CONFORMING THE CHURCH
           TO THE MODERN WORLD

1. The Justification of the World by the Church   13

    Jesus Christ, Lord of the World, 13
    Jesus Christ, Lord of History, 19
    The "No" and the "Yes," 23
    Some Examples of Justification, 26
    Involved in the World, 37

2. Making the Church Worldly   44

    The Christian, Man of the World, 45
    Adapting Christianity to the World's
        Thinking, 55

* * *

3. A Sociological Examination of Conscience   72

* * *

PART II: MAKING THE CHURCH POLITICAL

4. Clarifying Certain Preliminaries   89

Evidences of Political Involvement, 91
Causes of the Political Transformation, 100
The Biblical Question Mark, 109
Historical Metamorphoses, 117

5. How Choices Are Made   128

The Stated Motives, 129
The Real Motives, 140

6. Incompetence and Irresponsibility   153

Incompetence, 154
Fluctuations, 162
Irresponsibility, 169

* * *

7. The Orientation of Christians   176

*FALSE
PRESENCE
OF THE
KINGDOM*

Introduction

Christians in our day have become aware of a great truth: that the Church cannot live turned in upon herself and for herself. She is only the Church when she is sent into the world on behalf of mankind. It is basic, superb, that one should recollect and be convinced that you cannot have the Church on the one hand and mission or evangelizing on the other. Stated simply, whenever one sets out to separate these two terms, one denies the reality both of the Church and of evangelization. To speak of an "evangelizing Church" is to indulge in a tautology, for if there is no mission to the world, there is no Church.

From that fresh start, there is a tremendous burst of good will in our churches, in the more progressive movements, to insure this presence in the world. It has been said, and quite rightly, that Christians are rediscovering the vocation of the Church.

But the world in which we are living is very complex. It raises difficult questions, sets up barriers and lays numerous traps. Above all else, this world is terribly new. To insure a true presence, much more is required than good will and zeal, however Christian these may be. One can say, of course, that it is only necessary to become involved. The Holy Spirit will then take care of everything. But that seems to me to be a theological error. God has always required that man make use of his human equipment and knowledge. When we take stock of the actual forms and results of the presence in the world which Christians are attempting, we are obliged to ask ourselves whether the Holy Spirit has indeed offset the obvious defects of these good intentions.

The few suggestions which I set forth in *The Presence of the Kingdom* have clearly seemed much too intellectualized and difficult. The usual orientation is toward efforts at a presence much more simple, within the reach of everybody and more obvious. Now it does not seem to me that such a mode of proceeding has in any way insured a witness to faith in the lordship of Jesus Christ and in the salvation made available to all mankind. To the contrary, many of the commitments which appear to me to be mistaken are causing great disorder, confusion and sometimes scandal within the Church.

It is too simplistic to retort: "The traditional, backward and bourgeois Church troubled? So much the better!" In many instances it is a quite true and genuine faith that is beguiled into scandal. In other instances the reason for the confusion does not seem to be a particularly just and true display of renewed faith.

In the pages which follow I attempt the difficult and

formidable critique of the manifold involvements of these recent years. If I do so, it is not in the spirit of criticism and conflict. I would much prefer not to engage in the painful inquiry. On the one hand, I am convinced that we are on the wrong track in some of the involvements and that when all is said and done no presence in the world is guaranteed by this route. Yet my conviction alone would not be enough, because I may be mistaken. On the other hand, there is manifest danger for the Church and suffering for many Christians who do not understand.

The problem, then, is to determine whether it is legitimate to expose the Church to these dangers and our brothers to this suffering. If one is acting in truth, if one is bearing genuine witness to Jesus Christ, I would certainly answer "Yes." But if one is committed on the basis of false theological data or a false assumption about society, if there is a lack of clear-headedness or a cavalier approach, then surely the Church should be warned and protected.

This brings me to the following preliminary remarks, which for me are decisive:

(1) I am trying to describe a *factual* situation in the Reformed Church of France. It is not a matter of theological research. It is not a matter of describing what "ought to be," as though such a thing existed. Many "position papers," for example, are theologically well-founded, but the conclusions drawn from them and the behavior of their authors are often quite at variance with the stated theology. On the whole, it can be said that the theological renewal has won over almost the entire Church, and I personally am full of joy and gratitude for that setting forth of the truth. But it is equally

plain that a good theology is no guarantee of good conduct nor of an accurate view of the world. From a good
theology, alas, one can extract a dubious ethic, which,
moreover, soon reacts against the theological premises
and distorts them.

(2) I am trying to describe a *current* factual situation. For that reason I shall not enter upon a criticism
of the Church of a half-century or a century ago. That is
a criticism which one finds everywhere. All the writing
abounds in attacks against the bourgeois Church of the
nineteenth century, the Church without a mission, the
conformist Church, Protestant individualism, etc., and
we have had enough of that. Those criticisms are dis-
tasteful to me because, in effect, they imply that while
yesterday's Christians were wrong we, of course, are on
the path of the good, of truth and of righteousness. Obviously it is much easier to denounce the errors of the
past than to look for those of today.

I agree entirely with the judgments against the
Church of the nineteenth century, or even that of 1920,
but I am not at all certain that it is our business to try
those cases at a time when we have the task of criticizing
ourselves. Those mistakes of the past interest me only to
the extent that they are a warning and a lesson for us.
But then that implies that we have to ask ourselves
whether we are not, in our own day and *in relation to
the society and thinking of 1960,* committing the same
mistakes as the Church of 1860 may have committed in
relation to the society and thinking of 1860. Is it not
true that our insights into the Church of 1860 result
simply from the fact that society has changed?

(3) However stern my inquiry may occasionally
seem, it is not carried out in a spirit of condemnation,

still less in a spirit of superiority or of an easy conscience. I share in all the Church's errors. I suffer from
each one of these lapses and I accuse myself first of all.
If I write, it is not in order to wash my hands of the
matter and to get myself off scot-free.

It is rather that, living by the very life of the Church,
I feel myself affected by everything which looks to me
like compromise or error. If I stood apart I would not
suffer nor feel the need to call attention to these dangers. If I accuse myself first of all, it is not in a theoretical or general way. It is because, for the most part, I
have had those experiences myself. I have travelled
those same paths. I have been a victim of those same
errors and illusions in which I see many of our movements caught up. In several instances I personally bear
the responsibility for the involvement. So in each of
these exposés it is a matter first of all of a criticism of
myself.

(4) When I speak here of the Church, I obviously
am not thinking of the theological being of the Church
but of her human reality (albeit I am well aware that
the two cannot be separated. Praise God for that!).
Within this human reality I am thinking less of the
mass of the faithful in the congregations, who remain
level-headed for the time being. I am thinking rather of
the leaders of the Church, of the activist movements
and most of all of those in authority who speak and
write in the name of the Church, of the intellectuals.
My critique is based upon articles in Protestant magazines and newspapers, on resolutions of synods and congresses, on the personal acquaintance which I may have
in a given case.

I wish, therefore, to testify that what follows is not a

personal impression of the contemporary life of the Church, or an unfounded, embittered criticism, or an expression of resentment. Everything I set forth I could support by numerous citations, by specific examples and even by statistics! I have all that. Only rarely shall I offer such proof, for I do not wish to be heavy-handed and there is never any question of a personal quarrel. There is no passing of judgment on my brothers. It is purely a matter, in connection with a given account or a given observation, of discerning the overall trend and of putting the question of its validity and significance. That is why, whenever I make use of citations, I do not identify the authors. I consider that these statements have to do with the Church, with the thought and responsibility of the Church, and are not personal.

(5) For me it is a matter of trying to see clearly. Since the method is to be critical, I know that the accusation of pessimism and negativism will be leveled. To begin with, I would like to say that an examination of conscience never seems to me negative or pessimistic. Likewise the attempt to see clearly and to bring things into focus is never pessimistic or negative (even when it results in criticism!). I do not claim to be giving an account of *all* the contemporary life of the Church, as I have already indicated above. I leave deliberately to one side tremendous positive aspects of which I am fully aware. But in the presence of danger to warn of that danger, to call attention to that mistake on finding that we are on the wrong track, that appeals to me as being eminently positive and constructive.

On the other hand, it is true that I do not offer any solution in these pages. That is not because the "denunciation of error" seems to me to be sufficient (but again,

it is not a question of denunciation!). I have no solution. I could, of course, restate the theological ground-
work found in numerous scholarly writings, but the
next step is still uncertain. I might indicate some theoretical solutions, theoretical because not applicable to
the Church today. Such an approach would produce a
book much more satisfying and reassuring to the mind
of the reader, but that, for me, would be hypocritical
and dishonest. What I can say is that this examination
of conscience follows my work, *The Presence of the
Kingdom,* and precedes the work on *Christian Ethics* in
which I am now engaged. Let us assume that it is the
other way around.

Before undertaking this task, let us point out in a
general way some of the reasons for the difficulty in
which we find ourselves.

I am convinced of the profound reality of the theological awakening, of the earnestness of faith, of the
Church's recovery of vitality, of undoubted progress in
many spheres. There definitely is not a decline nor a
retrogression. There is a crisis which arises basically out
of the new theology, but it is a *positive* crisis.

Because of its very fidelity, the theology which we
may call "Barthian" makes difficult the approach to the
world and the formulation of an ethic. It accumulates
obstacles and problems, both intellectual and spiritual,
because that is the actual situation before God of the
man called by God. Here we derive no help from our
forefathers. We have to work our own way out of it. We
must find our own answers and open up our own paths.
But we shall never accomplish that if we run away from
the difficulty. In that case we would only be trapped

into conforming ourselves to our environment. (We shall go into detail about that later on.)

A second general cause stems from the newness of the world in which we are called upon to live. There again, we have to create, to innovate a form of Christian life in this world. The present world is without doubt one of the most complex in which man has ever found himself. Hence he is tempted to follow the world's leads, baptizing them in one way or another.

Finally, and again quite broadly, let us indicate a third factor, namely, the disappearance of Christendom (in the historic and sociological sense) and the advent of post-Christendom.* Here again, we are faced with a situation to which we are not accustomed and for which we are scarcely prepared. This is a good, and we can thank God for the liquidation of the era of Constantine and for the end to the monumental error which was Christendom (and we can really thank God for that, and God alone, for it was not by our virtue nor our clear-sightedness, nor by the faithfulness of Christians that Christendom was liquidated. It was, alas, by the external action of politics, of science, etc.). But we must realize that this brings us face to face with uncertainties. Again, the instinctive reaction will be to say: "Christendom is dead. Long live post-Christendom!"

Now in all this, a theology which is too good puts us

---

* The author's term *la chrétienté* has been translated *Christendom* throughout; his term *le christianisme* as *Christianity*. The author later describes the socio-historical structure of Christendom thus: "a vision of a society in which the political decisions, the social and economic structures, would be the fruit of the involvement of faith, to which all men can aspire, to which they can belong and in which they can all have a part on the strength of their natural reason."—Translator's Note.

in a certain position of weakness with respect to the world. The theology of Karl Barth is extraordinarily balanced. I believe it true precisely in the degree in which it expresses the remarkable dialectic that appears throughout the Bible, even in the least of its writings. But because all depends on this situation of tension, the elimination, or even the minimizing of one of the factors results in total and radical error, not just in a half truth. When the balanced tension, which is the visible sign of that theology, is broken, there is a collapse. We shall have occasion to give several examples of this. Here let us simply take note of a preliminary point. Theology has repeatedly recalled for us the rigorous transcendence of God, and rightly so. But that confronts us with the following twofold danger, to which we have seen most Protestant intellectuals succumb over the past fifteen years.

Sometimes one is led to put himself at the level of God, to judge events as though from the throne of God, to adopt the point of view of God himself. (I do not at all have in mind the same attitude as that of judgment *sub specie aeternitatis*. That is definitely not the same situation.) For example, one can write: "Alleluia, Jesus was crucified." Now that is a monstrosity. That God the Father, in his suffering, should have glorified his Son because the latter willed to give his life, so much is told us by scripture. But only God can do that. No man has the right to utter a cry of joy and victory because Jesus died on the cross, even when he knows that he owes his salvation to that death. This formula is no way to thank God for the saving sacrifice of his Son. It is a horrible presumption to consider the cross from the height of the divine throne.

The other error into which we are enticed by the accent on transcendence is the impossibility of communication between the will of the absolutely transcendent God and our concrete decisions. There was reason to criticize the famous pietistic concept of "the heavenly telephone," but when we are rudely reduced to our human condition on earth we have nothing to fall back on, neither a Christian morality, nor a simple explanation of the Bible in its literal sense, nor a continuing and inward inspiration of the Holy Spirit.

From that point on, we are left to our own responsibilities, which is all very well but by no means easy. We make our decisions, in effect, without reference to the content of revelation. Consequently, the determining factor of those decisions is the impact of sociology, politics and economics. Thus a theology in which one retains only the element of transcendence brings us remarkably into conformity with our milieu. This, without doubt, is the principal point of our present confusion and disorder.

PART ONE

Conforming the Church to the Modern World

1

The Justification of the World
by the Church

Man is justified by the grace of God in Jesus Christ.
That proclamation of Christian truth is not at issue
here. What is at issue is an error. Today's Christians,
thinking to succeed in being present to the world, try
their best to justify the world as it is.

JESUS CHRIST, LORD OF THE WORLD

The starting point for the logical construct is the
lordship of Jesus Christ. Jesus Christ has conquered the
world. He has stripped thrones, powers and dominions
of their pretensions and of their autonomy. He is now
and in actuality the Lord of the world and of history.

That is all quite right and basic, but there is drawn
from it a set of conclusions which are altogether wrong.
It is assumed that the works performed by man in this

world have henceforth become works that are valid, saved, and expressive of the will of the Lord. By the very fact of being performed, they become part of the plan and design of God. The Christian can only pronounce the great "Yes" of God over these works. He can only attest the good will of God, affirm that these works are a fulfillment and will become part of the Kingdom of God (often it is added that they prepare the way for it).

Thus human actions are positive actions and the Christian should take part in them, not as a last resort, not as in an absurd and meaningless world, but on the contrary, in a world which is positive, in a world in which the Christian cannot but reveal to those who make history the extent to which these works are worthy, valid and full of meaning before God because embraced within the lordship of Jesus Christ.

Therefore it is not for the Christian to "Christianize" the actions and works of secular man. He does not have a "Christian" work to do. He has only to take part in the works of men, of all men, precisely because, even when anti-Christian, it is those works which are under the lordship of Jesus Christ, which are ransomed (though men be unaware of it), and which are promised for the Kingdom of God. He has only to seek the good of the kingdom of man.

Henceforth the Christian man can (and *should*)— and this will be his true way of bearing witness—take part in the world of politics, in political action, in technological and scientific progress (without asking any questions about what is, and what is not, "permissible"), in economic works, etc. The Christian need not be

concerned whether a given act might be satanic (Satan
has been vanquished). He need not trouble himself
with the problem of good and evil. He should conduct
himself in full Christian liberty, taking part in every activity which is *positive* and *constructive* of tomorrow's
world. Since Christ has liberated him, he need not be
tied down by a set of paralyzing laws. Rejecting whatever has been superseded (for example, capitalism and
colonialism), he should move in the direction of building the world (for example, socialism and national independence). Performing in this way a work on behalf
of man, he accomplishes at the same time something
which enters into the plan of God.

God in Jesus Christ has pronounced the "Yes" over
every man's work, and we have only to repeat that
affirmation. By the resurrection, God has barred the road
to everything which is negative and dead. Through the
obedience of his Son, God has rendered disobedience
impossible. Where sin increased, grace abounded all the
more. Finally, let us recall in passing that this premise
leads to the conclusion that there is no frontier between
the Church and the world, and that the significant
greatness in all this is the world and the activity of men
in the world.

That is a very summary outline. There are dozens of
articles and books setting forth these ideas, but more
importantly there are an infinitely greater number of
articles and books written with these ideas presupposed,
without their being explicitly stated. Often these are
based directly on propositions of Karl Barth, but always following the same procedure of separating those
propositions from their counter-propositions, which

leads to serious errors. Indeed this set of conclusions drawn from the lordship of Jesus Christ seems to me to be an ensemble of clumsy theological mistakes.

It must be remembered that the lordship of Jesus Christ over the world does not at all signify a restoration of the creation to its integrity. The world is no more restored in its concrete existence than I cease to be a sinner because pardoned, or than I cease to be mortal because risen in Christ. With respect to the world and its political and technological works, we are today witnessing an error identical with the periodically recurring error which supposes that the assurance of the resurrection must make mankind immortal. The fact that Jesus Christ is truly the Lord of the world in no way guarantees that the works performed by man in this world are expressions of that lordship, or that they are entirely dedicated to salvation, and therefore that we can participate in them wholeheartedly and without reservation.

The world is still the world. The entire Gospel of John is there to testify to that. The world is a hostile power in revolt. It is too easy, and in fact false, to go so far as to say that the society, the environment in which we are living, is not "the world." Indeed it is! The political, economic and technological world is the world which the Gospel of John speaks of as radically lost, radically the enemy of God: and its works are not good works. The Prince of this world is still Satan. He wields an extraordinary power even when vanquished, as Oscar Cullmann reminds us. When Satan proposes to Jesus Christ to turn over to him the dominion over all the kingdoms of the world he is not lying. He continues to have authority over the political powers, and Jesus in no way disputes that point with him.

I am well aware of the objection which consists in saying that that has all been superseded, that beyond death there is the resurrection and beyond the power of the Prince of this world there is the power of *Christ Pantocrator*. But to pretend to extract from that indisputable truth *direct* consequences immediately applicable to action in contemporary society, *as is being done all the time,* is to fall into another error which the Church, for her part, has known too well. We might call this error that of the "already brought to pass," in the last analysis a theology of glory. But it involves a very strange theology of glory, for it is the glory of the world.

One reasons as though the Kingdom of God were already realized, as though it had already arrived, were already fulfilled, as though we were living in this Kingdom of God, as though all the actions of men were already registered in this Kingdom, present in its plenitude and effectively *replacing* the reality of the world. The optimism toward the works of man (once again on condition that they are "progressive!") implies that we are faced with a sort of unreserved approval on the part of God, and with a current actualizing, not of grace but of the plenitude of the works of grace. The entire dimension of hope is, in fact, canceled out.

I am aware, to be sure, that these same intellectuals will say that it is precisely because they have this hope that they act in this way and are optimistic. Yet, as a matter of fact, all the conclusions they draw imply that for them the whole weight is on the concept of the "already accomplished." In place of the tension between

the two inseparable terms of the "already accomplished" and the "not yet brought to pass" they substitute (without in fact saying so!) the single proposition
of the "already realized."

In so doing, one makes the same mistake as that made
in the Roman Church under another terminology.
What was lost in the fall was grace, a supernature. Nature itself is intact. Consequently the works of man are
to all intents and purposes good. In any case they can,
by natural means, be brought into conformity with the
divine plan. On the individual level one concludes with
the fact that original sin was washed away in and of itself by baptism, and that the person, from that moment
on, was restored to his state of innocence.

Now, starting from totally different premises, we arrive at the same result. Since the lordship of Jesus
Christ is contemporary, since the Kingdom of God is
present, all the works of *natural* man, of non-Christian
man, are inscribed in this merciful plan of God, and
hence they come into conformity with what he expects
of us. On the individual level, after a harsh criticism
and rejection of the idea of original sin, one is reduced
to saying that man is merely *fallible,* which comes to the
same thing in the end as the Catholic proposition.

If one is led into this twofold error, it is for the *same
reasons* which progressively motivated the Catholic theologians. "We have to manage to live in this world. We
must legitimize what is done by man. Life would indeed be monstrous and unbearable if all is destined for
destruction, if we are reduced to that negativism, if
nothing that we do makes any sense. We must reinstate
a 'possibility' for natural—or pagan—man. Only in
terms of that possibility can one take any action in poli-

tics, science or the economy. Otherwise it is useless to bother with anything."

If I summarize the attitude, the idea itself is not gratuitous. That the theologians were led, in one case as in the other, to find a theological expedient for legitimizing the works of man in the world was brought about by the necessity or the (legitimate) determination of Christians to participate in the life of the world. The Church faced the problem the moment it became evident that the end of the world was not going to happen right away. In that case, how do you live and participate in this pagan world which keeps on going? The same question faces us today, with respect to the neopagan world which is establishing itself. How do we live and participate in it, since that is our factual situation?

JESUS CHRIST, LORD OF HISTORY

A second very obvious error derives from the idea that Christ is the Lord of history, which leads us to affirm that history is a positive category, having its end-result in the Kingdom of God.

There is a serious, long-standing (and I hope unintentional) failure to distinguish between that history of which Christ is the Lord and the political and economic paths wherein we think to make history. It is a confusion between the lordship of Jesus Christ over history and the meaning given to history by a Marxist philosophy, for example. It is a confusion between the spread of the Kingdom of Heaven, of which the parables speak, and man's progress in history. It is a confusion between the end of that history in the merciful hands of the Lord and arriving at a technological or socialist paradise.

Again, even when one does not accept with enthusiasm the anti-Christian lucubrations of Teilhard de
Chardin, showing the normal, scientific and evolution-
ary end-result of history as the omega point, and how
collectivization is a step toward achieving this omega
point (!); even then, history, the domain of the changeable, the relative and the contingent, is habitually
transformed in modern discourse into a value, a power
which bestows value, and a kind of absolute. It is splendid to have rediscovered that God has revealed himself
in the course of a history and in history. It is horrible
to turn this humility of God into a theme of pride for
the history of man. Let no one object that the disserta-
tions of our philosophers and theologians are not so
crude as all that! As a matter of fact, under a very
complex vocabulary and with much confused reasoning,
that is exactly what they add up to.

Now, from the biblical point of view, the march of
history definitely does not end in this glory. The events
of history do not, of themselves, fulfill the plan of God.
God has intervened in the course of history, but the latter goes its own way, and that is not, in itself, the lordship of Jesus Christ. Economic laws, sociological laws
and the landmarks of history are neither a progress toward the Kingdom, nor signs of the action of the Lord
in history.

There is a great temptation today to confuse
sociological evolution with spiritual progress, and
Christians are the first to succumb to that temptation.
Nevertheless the Bible expressly tells us that the history
of mankind ends in judgment. It does not give place to
the Kingdom. It destroys itself in the judgment, which
is not a sham nor a myth. There is no continuity be-

tween our history and the Kingdom, any more than there is a continuity between our earthly life and our resurrected life. We must pass through death and destruction. All the historic works of man, technological, scientific and artistic, go down into the annihilation which is the end of the judgment, when the flaming elements will dissolve into nothing.

To be sure, as I have already written, God in his mercy saves man with his works. That is to say that on the other side of death there is indeed the resurrection. On the other side of the judgment there is grace. Consequently the history of man is saved along with man, and the works of man are taken up by God, made use of by him for his Heavenly Jerusalem, and that is a matter of grace pure and simple. God does not receive these works because they are valid, but because man, saved in Jesus Christ by grace, is saved in his totality. But this means that history has no pre-eminent or exceptional value. History has no privileged significance. It is nothing but a sort of appendage to man. Man is the important thing, not history. The latter exists because man lives, and history adds no value whatsoever to man.

On the other hand, just as we do not know how we shall be resurrected, nor what we shall be in the resurrected life (1 Corinthians 15), so also we can say absolutely nothing concerning the meaning of the "recapitulation of history in Christ," or how our destroyed works will be taken up by God. There will be all the distance indicated to us by the Bible between the contemporary Jerusalem and the Heavenly Jerusalem.

Hence we are absolutely incapable of forming any idea of the current validity of our works of civilization, or of the good to be derived from Christian participation in them. The fact that from now on Jesus Christ is Lord surely means that from now on there is a new order within the world's disorder. In the same way, also, there is a new man born in each one of us, but we would be presumptuous to suppose that this new man is purely and simply our present being in its entirety!

Now this mysterious order, this Kingdom of Heaven, as big as a grain of mustard seed, hidden like a treasure in a field, unseen, we can only belong to by an explicit adherence which is that of faith. One does not share *implicitly* in this new order, which is that of Jesus Christ, simply by acting like everyone else in the performance of one's professional or political duties. One shares in it by the acknowledgment with mouth and heart that Jesus Christ is the Lord.

✓ The tendency today is excessively to minimize the importance of the faith. With many of our intellectuals one gets the impression that since Jesus Christ is Lord, therefore all men, whatever their religion or intention, share in that order and their works are within the lordship of Jesus Christ. But the scriptures, on the contrary, insist on the fact that the acceptance of this new order is deliberate and intentional. Otherwise we are on the way to reviving the medieval heresy of "implicit faith!"

Even though Christ is the Lord, the works of man are still works of darkness, and the only thing which signifies the lordship of Christ is the receiving of the Kingdom of Heaven in faith. It goes without saying that God makes use of the sputnik and of the communists, just as he made use of the Assyrians and the Egyptians, but that does not mean that the communists do good works, any more than did the Assyrians, about whom the prophets tell us quite enough!

THE "NO" AND THE "YES"

A third error, connected with the two preceding ones, stems from the separation, in fact if not in word, between the "No" and the "Yes." One is generally in agreement with the Barthian statement that, just as God pronounced over his Son the "No" of the judgment and of death and the "Yes" of the resurrection and the glorification, so also has he made these pronouncements over every man and over all the works of man. But throughout the literature it turns out, as a matter of fact, that since the "Yes" is ultimate, since it comes *after* the "No," since the "Yes" is the source of hope, since the "Yes" corresponds to the Gospel, one simply cancels out the "No," and pays no further attention to it. Just as in former times the Church spoke exclusively of the "No," so today we limp with the other foot.

It is not exact to say that, since death has been swallowed up, one can live as though there were no death, or that, since grace abounds, all the possibilities of progress are open to us! We need to maintain a rigorous dialectic. The "Yes" of God is pronounced in relation to a previous "No." Without the "No," there is no "Yes," and the "No" in question is not a mere "manner of speaking," a mere "appearance" (like that heresy which claimed that the death of Jesus was only a seeming), nor a superseded moment of time (the death of Jesus a bad moment!). But just as repentance has always to be renewed in the Christian life, just as we have ever anew to find ourselves under judgment, just as Christ is crucified to the end of the world, just so the

"No," pronounced by God over man and his works and his history, is a "No" which is total, radical and ever present.

The "Yes" of God is not a cancellation, an erasure of the "No," as it would appear to be throughout the writings of our Protestant intellectuals. The work of man is always under the "No," which is absolutely real. The death of Jesus Christ, the judgment of the Father on the Son, the "My God, why?", these are terrible realities, absolutely devastating for us. Likewise our death and our judgment are real, serious and terrible.

So also the annihilation of works and of history is a genuine and total annihilation. We cannot minimize it by saying: "Yes, but *afterward* . . .", for it is God who pronounces that *afterward,* and not we. When Jesus was dead in the tomb it was not he who raised himself again. It was God who raised him. To calculate: "Yes, but afterward"—since one is too good a theologian—is to mistake oneself for a *deus ex machina.* We must, on the contrary, maintain the dialectic of the "No" and the "Yes," which allows of no speculation about progress, or about history, or about successful participation in the political works of man today.

Whenever we think, for example, of a given political problem, we truthfully have no right to dissociate the positive from the negative passages in the Bible (letting the negative ones drop). When we appeal to people, it is not merely to assure them of God's great "Yes" over their lives and work. That "Yes" makes no sense unless there is also the "No," and I regret to point out that the "No" comes *first,* that death comes before resurrection. If the "No" is not lived in its reality, the "Yes" is a nice pleasantry, a comfort which one adds to one's material comfort, and as Barth has conclusively shown, the "No" is *included* in the Gospel.

It is not a question of pronouncing a judgment of discrimination between good works and bad works (which is ruled out by the parable of the wheat and the tares). This "No" and this "Yes" apply to every human undertaking and to every man. The "No" is against the world's enterprise, which moves toward judgment and death. The "Yes" is for the work of God, to which we look in hope, and which ends with the taking up of the work of man. One cannot really proclaim the Gospel without also proclaiming the "No" included in it, and which is also itself a gospel.

But, obviously, man expects something quite other than that from the Church! When it is said that we should give people what they expect of us, I am puzzled; it is as though man were not fundamentally a sinner, as though he were looking for the good news of God's forgiveness! To evangelize from the standpoint of such ideas gives rise, necessarily, to serious misunderstandings, and that, moreover, is what we see occurring.

What does man expect?—quite simply that the Church, speaking for God, should tell man that he is right—quite simply that one should proclaim "Jesus' faith in man." In that case man can calmly go back to his business and act as he sees fit! In his eyes the Church is there to provide him with justification, but not, of course, the justification which Jesus Christ provides! When kings turned to the Church, it was to have theologians explain to them what superb kings they were, and how their works enjoyed the approval of God. When the bourgeoisie went to church, it was to hear it said that their work was blessed by God and that riches were a sign of grace. When the communists today lay such store by the alliance with Christians, it is (in addition to other reasons which we shall come upon later) out of the same motivation.

The Church makes us right. Our undertakings are justified by Christianity. It is the traditional role of the Church to affirm that God agrees with what man is concocting. Time was when we had a good laugh at the Catholic church for blessing fishing fleets, packs of hounds and cages of bears. Now it is exactly that same stance which we are in process of adopting when we declare that the sputnik, automation or television are splendid inventions, part of the plan of the Creator, and that the Church should of course pronounce the great "Yes" of God over these works of man.

SOME EXAMPLES OF JUSTIFICATION

Without entering into the political domain, which we reserve for later on, there are abundant examples to show how Protestant intellectuals and numerous theologians today are given to justifying whatever modern man is in process of doing, and how they devote a good part of their writing to showing that it is all right. The rational demonstrations, which of course contain their share of theological argument, frequently tailored to suit the occasion, never fail to include a condemnation of the concepts of the Church of yesterday, and of the life-style of yesterday's society.

We shall tarry briefly over the question of technology. Christians, like everyone else in our society, are enthusiastic about technology. It affords a good example, for it gives rise to a whole theological literature demonstrating that in modern technology man is being true to the purposes of God, and that it is justified from a theological as well as from a scientific point of view. Broadly speaking, there are two arguments put forward.

One is based on the vocation which man is supposed to have received from God, which the Catholic theologians call "the demiurge function." Protestant theologians dare not go so far as to call it that, but in reality what they say amounts to the same thing. In the creation, God assigned to man the role of implementation and of dominion. Reference is made, of course, to Genesis 1 and 2, as well as to Psalm 8, which can be used in many ways.

From these descriptions one derives the idea, which is not there originally, that man was given a function of organization, exploitation and utilization. With that beginning, one moves on to the complementary idea of adding to what already exists. Hence, today's technological progress is simply the application of the vocation which God gave to man. Through technology, man is using to the limit that which God has placed at his disposal, and he is demonstrating his dominion over the creation.

But in order to arrive at these conclusions, one has to make deductions which are not legitimate. It is distinctive in Genesis that work is described as useless work and that the idea of dominion does not automatically imply organization or technological exploitation.

In addition, one has to suppress, unwarrantedly, the reality of the alienation from God, and to treat what is said in Genesis 1 and 2, or in Psalm 8, as though it were applicable to man today, forgetting about Genesis 3. One has to shut one's eyes to the difference between the

order given to Adam in the creation and the order
given in the covenant with Noah. In the order of the
fall, which is not that of the creation, man dominates by
fear. He does violence to the creation which is "delivered" into his hands (Genesis 9).

Finally, one has to shut one's eyes to the explicit biblical teaching on the origin of technology. To complete
all this changeover, one makes use of the concept of
myth and of phenomenological categories, whereby it is
possible to eliminate from the texts all the passages
which are embarrassing to the operation. But the aim
and the fundamental motive underlying this false exegesis is that of justifying the activity of man in modern society.

The other theological argument, which is a sequel to
this, consists in saying that, in effect, the work of God
was not complete, not consummated, not finished at the
time of the creation told about in Genesis. The proof
alleged is that the work only received its fullness in
Jesus Christ. Hence there had to be this guilt. Sin has a
plus sign, since it caused on the one hand the forward
movement of history, which is a positive movement end-
ing in the Kingdom of God, and on the other hand it
caused the incarnation of Christ. The new Adam is
infinitely superior to the first Adam, and the Kingdom
of God is infinitely superior to Eden. Now the forward
movement of history is fulfilled in technology. Man
brings a perfection to the primitive work of God, by
opening it out, explaining it and raising it to a higher
level. Therefore it is that work of man which makes
possible the final completion of the creation.

Here again, we should note a definite conflict with
scripture. There we are told that the creation was com-

pleted, that it was perfect and that there was nothing to add to it (Genesis 1). Moreover, Christ was already the perfection of that creation. He was already the true and perfect image of God. He was already its fullness. The terrible course of events in which man involved God added nothing to that fullness. The manifestation of God's love in the sacrifice of his Son adds nothing to that love, nor to the creation. All that was antecedent.

Finally, it is to be remembered even so, that if the work of man and the history of man are taken up by God and recapitulated in the glorified Christ, that is definitely not because they are valid, not because they make a positive contribution to improve that which God had willed, but because, in his love, God saves man *with* his works. It is by grace that he transforms evil into good, and wills indeed to take into account what man has done. The new creation is not superior to the first by the addition of the work and history of man, but by a new achievement of the love of God.

It is shameful to have to recall that, biblically, sin presents no positive aspect whatsoever. To deduce this positive quality through theological reasoning proves only that there has been a theological error somewhere. Sin is exclusively separation from God, hence separation from life, from truth, from the good. Once again, this theological endeavor has only one goal, to justify the work of man. Of course one insists, against Catholicism, that every work of man is under the sign of sin, but as one cannot bring oneself to treat all this work as evil before God, one has to find some way to attribute a positive quality to sin!

Nevertheless, we should remember that the more one attributes value to man and his works, the more one de-

values God and his love. It is a very old story, which formerly took place on the moral plane, and which today
takes place on the level of the technological experience,
for that is the great work of man. Man, today, wants at
all costs to save this great work and to proclaim it just
and good—and, as though by accident, the theologians
follow that line.

Now, quite obviously, this determination to justify
modern man is the opposite to proclaiming his justification in Christ. The justification in Christ implies the
journey toward death and to the core of evil. It implies
the impossibility of man's performing any work whatsoever which is valid before God. It implies recognition
that it is indeed *in Christ* that we are justified. However, what the above methods of justification introduce
is the maneuver which man over and over again tries to
use: that of declaring himself righteous independently
of Christ; and here the theologians provide modern
man with the means of declaring himself righteous in
his works, in his technology.

Of course the theologian will protest, saying: "But
that only has to do with the problem of man's finitude.
It does not refer to his justification." Or perhaps: "But
you must understand all that 'in Christ'!" As a matter
of fact, however, modern man does not understand it
that way. What he has in mind is that his work is accepted and justified in advance. We should note, moreover, that modern man (unless he is a "Christian") will
not very often make use of what the theologians try to
put at his disposal, for he has much more effective ways
of justifying himself! The only thing he will think is
that, after all, the Christians agree with him.

We could multiply these samples of "new" theological argument ("new" in form, but how old-fashioned in intention!) which are meant to justify nearly all the elements, all the ideas, all the works of the modern world. One need only scan newspapers, magazines and lectures.

One of the great myths of the modern world is that of *work*. Leaving out of account a whole segment of the biblical revelation, one concentrates solely on the positive quality, on the passages which indicate that work is good, while rejecting its character as punishment, as duty, as pain, as a mark of the status of sinfulness and of subjection to necessity. It can be said, alas, that if the Church of the Middle Ages in general (not at Citeaux!) taught only the punitive and chastising aspect of work, that was because such was the opinion current at that time, an opinion which stemmed from the Roman as well as from the Germanic background. Alas, it can also be said today that if one sets forth the character of work as something positive and required before God, that is because modern man lives in the myth of work created by the bourgeoisie of the seventeenth and eighteenth centuries and adopted enthusiastically by contemporary neo-socialism.

Similarly, modern man makes happiness the primary aim of life, and how many articles have we seen written by Christians expressing approval of that principle, saying that the use of the world's goods for the sake of happiness is in the divine order, that the pursuit of happiness is entirely legitimate, that the Church of former times was quite wrong in presenting asceticism and a limitation on the consumption of goods as Christian modes of conduct, that she was wrong in condemning the search for happiness as a "friendship with the world" and as a pagan attitude. Unfortunately, I would be tempted to say that the Church taught asceticism in a time of economic scarcity, just as today she teaches happiness in a time of an increase in the standard of living. She obeys the demand of the times.

In the intellectual sphere, we witness the same temptation. We have been good at criticizing the stand of Catholic scientists striving to demonstrate that a given scientific discovery is in harmony with Christian principles (for example, the undertakings of Le Comte du Nouy, and the utilization of the discoveries of Planck and of Heisenberg), but we fall into the same trap ourselves. Taking modern philosophical investigations, we adopt the existential or the phenomenological view of man and conclude by saying: "Wonderful! We have come around once again to the Christian view of man!" So we proceed exactly like the Catholics we had criticized, and we do it by a sort of reversal of direction. On the one hand, with a Christian concept in the backs of our minds, we employ philosophy. On the other hand, rediscovering a given aspect of Christianity (frequently in a very modified form, for we think to explain theology through philosophy), we make use of it to justify modern philosophy's being what it is.

In the same way one justifies the modern myth of history, the monumental importance assumed by history today from the fact of historical science and from the Hegelian-Marxist thinking. An entire segment of Protestant writing today tends to show that such an interpretation of man and of the world is good, just and exact, that we *must* adopt the world's categories of thought because they are justified. We have already indicated the rudiments of this question.

Finally, as a last example out of hundreds, is the justifying attitude of numerous Christians toward anti-Christian movements. One could cite a number of passages of which the general theme is that, in the last analysis, the contemporary world is quite right in being what it is, and that all the evil is concentrated in the Church. People are anti-Christian? It doesn't occur to our authors that such could *also* (I do not say *only!*) be what the Bible is telling us: the hate which natural man has against those who preach the Gospel, the sinful rejection of the preaching of the truth, the satanic persecution of the people of God, the perverse will to destroy the bearer of witness.

No, no! If there be anti-Christians, it is solely because Christians are hypocrites and horribly bourgeois, because the Church is bogged down in her institutions, because the Gospel is not preached and lived in its purity (odd theology, which leads to the supposition that natural man would receive the Gospel like a good little lamb if the Gospel were rightly preached). The condition for the Gospel's being received is that Christians should "share in the human adventure." Moreover, "in reality, it is the Church which needs to be evangelized by the world" (which is stupid!). Nowhere in scripture is it the world which is charged with preaching the good news of the death and resurrection of Jesus Christ. Now, what is more, it is also alleged that the Kingdom is only manifested "through the mediation of the least Christians in any case"!! These contentions, alas, are not paradoxes, but adoration of the world.

It is not a matter of my justifying the Church or Christians; and even now I am attacking ourselves! But it is not reasonable to go so far as to justify anti-Christian movements. I am not referring to our taking seriously a profound and genuine (scientific or philosophic) attack upon our faith or upon our attitudes. I believe we should listen to whatever historical or sociological criticism, or Nietzsche, or Marx have to say in condemning us. I take my stand, on the one hand, on the level of the justifications which we bestow upon "the world," and, on the other hand, on the level of movements and institutions. That the acceptance of condemnation could be a sign of humility, a possibility for involvement or dialogue, a test of faith willed by God, that is all well and good, but it in no way entails the proclamation that the persecutors of the Church are right!

Let us recall the Chaldean, an agent of God for the chastising of Israel. That is how he is announced and described *to the people of God* by the prophet. But the prophet also announces his condemnation and ruin, precisely for having acted against those who are, *nonetheless,* the people of God (Isaiah 10:5ff.; Jeremiah 25 and 50). Israel's disobedience does not justify the Chaldean in being what he is. So it is today!

Quite contrary to this, we are now seeing Christians welcoming with open arms everything in the nature of an attack against Christianity and the Church. Mme de B . . . tells us that Christianity is a slimy hypocrisy? "She is right!" Psychologists say that faith is nothing but a substitute for repressed sexual impulses? "Well said!" A government deports Christians, imprisons bishops and tortures priests? "Good! At last there will be no more compromise of conscience, and this is proof that the clergy were in league with capitalists." The government is about to suppress Christian schools? "Why, of course. That helps our cause." (That is what the Church in

Hungary said in 1955, when one-third of the faculties of theology were eliminated.)

One gives his allegiance to the party which openly proclaims its opposition to Christianity, etc. Everything which drags the Christian faith in the mud and tends to suppress the Church is received with joy. Conversely, all thinking which tries specifically to be biblical is treated as uninteresting, and anything the authorities of the Church might say on a given question is suspect and soon forgotten.

Now that attitude is not by any means the legitimate one, which consists in counting "it all joy . . . when you meet various trials" (James 1:2), that is to say, persecution. Even so, let us remember that in persecution the Church is holy to God, that the world acts as a power of darkness and, because it is darkness, it cannot but try to extinguish the light. Such is the meaning of persecution. But how can we support a regime which seeks the destruction of the Church in China, in North Viet Nam, in North Korea, or which seeks to purge it in Cuba or Yugoslavia, or to enslave it in the people's republics?

I know the answers which are given: that the bourgeois Church should disappear (but let us remember that bourgeois and unfaithful as she is, she is still the Church); that it is good to see disappear the sociological structures which sustain the Church artificially (but let us remember that the Church is also a human society which cannot dispense with structures, which suffers, and even cannot live, when its institution is destroyed); and that it is just as well that the Church should finally come really to know what it is to be beneath the cross (which is true, but that does not imply praise for those who drive the nails and plant the cross!). Still worse is it to justify this attitude on the ground that the Church must die (she to whom it was said that the gates of hell shall not prevail against her!), with a mistaken exegesis of Philippians 2 as a point of departure.

All this, again, is nothing but a justification of the works of the world. It becomes tragic when Christians support movements which have as their purpose the ruin of the Church, as was the case with the majority of German Protestants (foremost among them Niemoller*) toward Nazism in 1931-33, and as is the case with a great many Protestant intellectuals toward French communism, or toward the FLN, the organization for Algerian independence. Just as the Christian does not have the right before God to seek persecution at all costs, still less does he have the right to bring it on the Church by supporting her enemies. It is infantile to suppose that they would be disarmed by a display of good will, kindness and understanding.

But since one must expect all kinds of misunderstandings, I want to make it clear that when I emphasize the unacceptable character of this infatuation, which throws Christians into the arms of that which is most opposed to them (communism or Islam), it does not in the least mean that the opposite extreme, such as a crusade, has any place in my thinking. It is not the place of the Church to struggle against her enemies by force, either through the state or through the institution. But neither is it her place to aid her enemies in the political arena, nor to adopt their ideology.

---

* I cite this name only to the extent that Pastor Niemoller is often put forward as an *example* of political lucidity.

I further wish to make clear that I refer here to doctrine, to institutions, to movements, parties and states, not to persons. "Love your enemies" does not mean to me that we must love the demons and the powers in revolt, but rather people. Now many Christians succumb precisely to that temptation. They want to love the people who are the enemies of the Church, and with that in view they take on their way of thinking and acting, as well as their judgments, and they play into the hands of their party or nation. This is a tragic error and a spiritual misrepresentation. But still less is it a question of justifying a society which calls itself Christian, which ensnares the Church in complacency. It is true that we are in process of escaping that situation.

INVOLVED IN THE WORLD

The entire Bible tells us that Christians are called to be involved in the world. But again, we have to understand what is meant by that. We are there to give testimony about a justification which washes away sin but which never makes it legitimate.

To be present to the world does not at all imply doing the world's bidding, walking in its ways or reinforcing it. A favorite citation on this topic is Jeremiah's letter to the captives in Babylon (Jeremiah 29), but it is falsely applied. In the first place, no account is taken of the vast biblical thrust commanding us to flee the world, to reject it and even to condemn it. Then too, it is forgotten that if the captives were ordered to preserve the world, that was not for the benefit of the world, but because God wills the preservation of his people, whose material lot was bound up with that of Babylon. According to this passage, therefore, if one is to participate in the life of the world, *that is in order to maintain the Church.*

Now the world of which John, Paul, James or Peter speaks is, in spite of the distortions to which many of the passages are subjected, the world in which we are living: the political, economic and social world; the scientific, artistic and technological world in which man lives. It is partly the work of man and partly the work of demons, or of the powers, as we were reminding ourselves above. It is not at all an abstract, metaphysical notion.

To be present to the world does not mean being present on behalf of the world, but on behalf of the people who live in it (John 17:20). To attribute value to the world is to deny the incarnation. If God loved the world, it is because the world was not lovable and good. If God reconciled the world to himself, it is because the world was in a state of rebellion and rejection. But this loved and reconciled world is still the world. It is not yet the Kingdom. The works of the world remain works of darkness, but darkness into which a light has come, which does not validate or justify the darkness.

Frequent use has been made, in these latter days, of the idea that the Church should be converted to the world. That idea cannot be entertained. If it means merely that the Church should turn toward the world, should come out of her self-satisfaction, her obsession with herself, her contented purring, that is obvious. But why use the expression: "be converted"? It should be put alongside that other formula: "The Church is for the world." Here again, no! The Church needs only to be converted over and over again to her Lord, and she is

for people. Now she cannot be for people except where
they are, and that is in the world. So she must be in the
world and walking along with it, but not for the purpose of building the world as it builds and wants to
build itself.

The whole Bible tells us that these people in the
world are enslaved by the world. They belong to it.
They are the slaves of political, economic and intellectual forces. The Church is there to proclaim and to
bring them freedom. But if she is an agent of those
forces, and shares in them herself, she cannot be for
people at all. If she justifies the works of the world, she
is in no position to witness, on people's behalf, to the
justification in Christ. She becomes what she always
tends to become: one of the powers of the world.

When the clergy, in the year 1800, glorified work,
money, economic development and empire, they were
acting as men of their world and of their milieu. They
involved the Church with the bourgeoisie because they
were of the bourgeoisie themselves. When today's clergy
glorify work, democracy, socialism and technology they
are acting as men of their world and of their milieu.
Belonging to the new social category known as "the intellectual leaders," they adopt its imagery, vocabulary
and newspapers.

What I am saying does not at all imply that we are in
the world *in order to* object to it, to condemn it and to
refuse to live in it. If I affirm that the Christian is not
sent into the world in order to justify it, that definitely
does not mean that the right attitude would automatically be to take the opposite point of view! (I have
often said and written, for example, that the secularity
of the state, or conscientious objection, seemed to me to

be true aims to adopt in the world.) But we are present as representatives of the Wholly Other, to bring to the world what the world rejects and does not want to hear about.

Whenever we ponder the world's problems and strive to be active in the world, we must take as our point of departure one which is not, and which cannot be that of the present century, one which cannot send us down the path of approval of the steps taken by the world, because its sense of direction is radically different. It is a matter of bringing another viewpoint, another scale of values, another orientation, another goal to bear on those same problems and those same endeavors. It is at this point that we encounter the necessary presence together of the "No" and the "Yes."

Finally, being present to the world cannot imply the formula which has also created a furor, namely, "at the risk of losing oneself." The point of view is well known. It assumes that being present to the world, joining with the world, having Christians mingle with people is so important that it should be done even if the Christians themselves become lost. One should risk *all*. One points, of course, to the biblical examples of the salt and the leaven which are mingled with the soup or the dough. Many pretty and romantic statements have been made on that subject. What is more serious, in implementing the idea, many young people have been sent into dangerous commitments.

Now the formula itself is false and absurd. An involvement in the world *at the risk of losing oneself* means only that one is lost, but that neither the world nor the people in it have gained anything in the process. To accept perdition for oneself in advance with a view to saving the world involves a combination of theological and spiritual errors which I consider to be tragic.

In the first place, it is once again to put oneself in the place of God in Jesus Christ. Only God could love the world which is the enemy of God. Only Jesus Christ could lose himself for people (and moreover not for the world!). Only Jesus Christ could go down the road which is described for us in Philippians 2.* Paul does not say that we should follow *that* path (which, moreover, Jesus had told us that we are indeed incapable of following!), but rather that we should have in us the mind which was in Christ (which is quite a different matter), and then forthwith: *"work out your own salvation!"* Hence it is strictly impossible to interpret Philippians 2:12, as an invitation to lose ourselves in the world! Only Jesus Christ could lose himself in death, because only God could love to that extent. As for us: "remember that you were bought with a price."

To submit to losing the salvation obtained in Jesus Christ is precisely to scorn the entire work of Jesus Christ. It is to scorn the incarnation and crucifixion. It is to forget what it cost God to save each one of us. If, as Jesus tells us, there is joy in heaven over one sinner who repents, we should consider all the pain and misery there is in heaven over a righteous person who allows himself to be lost. No, none of us has the right, even for

* For the commentaries to remind us of the humility, the nakedness, the nonaggression, the self-emptying of the will to power is true, but well-known, traditional and commonplace. The imitation of Jesus Christ in the path of suffering has continually been urged by the Church. But to take from that a command to participate in political life, or in a sort of destruction of the Church, or any kind of identification of Christ and the Church is an abuse of language.

love, to rejoin the world at the risk of being lost himself. That would be to love one's neighbor more than God and more than oneself, which is the reverse of the order of love. That would also be to yield to the third temptation set before Jesus Christ (to obey the adversary in order to conquer the world for God).

I realize that one answer will be: "But you mustn't overstate the case. Since salvation depends on eternal election, a person does not risk being lost." I reply that, in that case, to broadcast the command: "Involve yourselves in the world to the point of risking being lost yourselves," while saying to oneself, "They aren't risking anything, since there is the election," seems to me to be a wretched prank and a dangerous act. If it is true that we cannot be the judges of their salvation, we can at least observe that there are young people committed on the basis of this formula who, when subjected to too great a test in the world, to too radical a confrontation, have given up confessing that Jesus Christ is their Saviour.

I also say that this formula is absurd. If the involvement in the world has any meaning, it is precisely that persons saved and regenerated by Jesus Christ should bear testimony concerning *that* salvation, and should live in the world as persons who are regenerated. Now if, in the name of love for the world, they submit to losing that salvation, they cannot live as witnesses to the Saviour, for they treat the salvation as a secondary matter.

Here is a true case of the salt which has lost its savor. You can always mix the savorless salt with food, and it doesn't accomplish a thing. To become of the world and to lose oneself in the world accomplishes nothing for people. To allow oneself to be damned out of love for the other person could eventually result in two damned people, never in one saved person!

It is a matter of mingling with the world while strictly refusing to be lost, while retaining the specific character, the uniqueness, of the truth revealed in Jesus Christ and of the new life we have received from him. It is a matter of supplying the savor of the salvation, of the truth, of the freedom and of the love which are in Christ, and never letting oneself be taken over by the perdition of the world, with its strength, its splendor and its efficiency! *

* I have taken some examples of slogans which are widely used in contemporary Protestantism. It is really a current fad to make use of propaganda slogans, which are suspect theologically, but which are "striking." For example: "The Church must die," "Worship is non-worship," "Jesus has faith in man," "The Church must let herself be evangelized by the world," etc. As a Protestant intellectual said to me: "The most important thing is to shock the hearer."

2

Making the Church Worldly

Not only do we see our Church tempted to resume the traditional attitude of justifying the world's works, but we also are witness to a variety of ways in which the Church is being made worldly.

The starting point for this temptation is an observation which, as usual, contains a half-truth. It goes like this: The Church is a closed environment, with well-known affiliations. It is an environment turned in upon itself, suffering from a minority complex, bound by tradition, jealously guarded about its Bible and proud of a moralism which is scornful of other people. If the Christian life is to make any sense, if the Christian and the Church are to have a missionary and an apostolic vocation, then Protestants must be brought out of their milieu and made to mingle with the world. They must free themselves from tradition and go out to meet others. "Come out of your shell!" is the proud slogan being spread abroad by many of the movements.

THE CHRISTIAN, MAN OF THE WORLD

Now such analysis of the Protestant situation, with its resulting proposal, is behind the times and partial. It is behind the times because it is true of Protestantism at the turn of the last century but not true of the Protestantism of 1960. It is partial because it is probably true of one portion of Mediterranean or of Parisian Protestantism but not true of the rest (and less and less true even of Parisian Protestantism). The Protestantism of the outlying districts and of the suburbs, the Protestantism of the displaced and of the younger generation no longer corresponds to that picture. But especially is there a failure to recognize the extent to which all Protestants are now conformed to the rest of mankind. Less and less is there a Protestant milieu, and there no longer exists a Protestant life style.*

What are Christians interested in? The content of the newspaper, television, one's own business and, incidentally, politics. In other words they are just like everyone else. There is nothing to point up their Christian faith. Obviously, in a period of great decadence, the Protestant was a person who stood out by reason of his superior austerity. He was scrupulously honest, strictly

---

* The sentiment of the Protestant ghetto is seldom felt by the faithful, only by the pastors. For those who, in fact, have contact only with church members, and who gravitate always toward the Protestant milieu, it is indeed conceivable that they should feel the need to escape, but they are making a great mistake when they suppose that their experience is standard.

bored on Sunday and dressed in black. Those outward
signs, together with the moralism, were, to be sure, for-
malities quite incidental to the Christian life, and it was
wrong to lay such great store by them. But having as-
sailed tradition and got rid of that pharisaism,* we have
replaced that life-style, which was but poorly, indif-
ferently and gloomily Christian, with what? With exactly nothing, and that does not seem to me to be a sign
of such great superiority. There is no life-style, neither
individual nor collective, which is showing forth the
Christian faith.†

The Protestant lives like everybody else, works like
everybody else, thinks like everybody else and reacts
like everybody else. He is seduced by technology. He
shares the same hopes and fears with everyone. He feels
crushed by the Algerian tragedy, lives through "eventu-
alities" emotionally and follows the news feverishly.
Thus he participates in the hopes and terrors of all.

If that is the way it is, let's not fool ourselves. It means
that this Christian is of the world. He is fed the same information and is subject to the same influences. He
belongs to the same organizations, is troubled in the
same ways and obeys the same reflexes as other people.

Let's not be too quick to think: So much the better!,
because in the end that does not mean that he has been
"sent into the world," as we would like to affirm, but it

* Got rid of it, moreover, for what motive? Is it so certain that it was
in order to show forth a more authentic faith? Was it not also a fact
that the world laughed at those Protestants and that, after all, not
everyone has the courage to wear a Salvation Army uniform?

† For we cannot speak of a showing forth of the faith when, for example, one joins a political party just like everybody else. Once again, the
problem would be to know why. But we shall be dealing with that
more fully.

means rather that he is of the world, which hardly seems compatible with the faith in Jesus Christ. To be sure, there is still a certain vocabulary left over (which one strives to purge away). There are certain wavering habits of piety* and an inward faith.

Do you want Christians to mingle with the world? That's an accomplished fact. All the faithful are so mingled. Do you want the Church to be open for the dispensing of her fruits in the world? The fact is that for a long time the Church has been nothing but an artificial gathering of essentially worldly people, which brings "the world" into the Church (without, unfortunately, bringing in people!). That is not altogether a thing to be desired. The problem is not at all: "Come out of your shell," but: "Given the fact that you are constantly immersed in this bath, what can being a Christian in it possibly mean?" (a question which the Association of Protestant Professionals [APP] have tried in vain to answer).

Christians who are conformed to the world introduce into the Church the value-judgments and concepts of the world. They believe in action. They want efficiency. They give first place to economics, and they think that all means are good (for the spread of the Church, goes without saying!). They are defined by their sociological milieu. The Protestant thinks to adopt the means which the world employs. Since he finds those means useful in his profession, or in his leisure time, they stand so high

---

* Whereas among Catholic youth there is a renewal of love for the Bible, it has to be acknowledged that among Protestant youth there is a disturbing lack of interest both in the personal reading of the Bible and in the group study of it, unless indeed the latter is given a definite political slant.

in his estimation that he cannot see why he should not introduce them into the Church and make the things of the spirit dependent upon them.

He never faces the problem of these means. They are there. They are effective. Hence they are good. Since they are in a sanctified world and are effective, why not make use of them in the Church? The criteria of his thinking as a Christian are so vague, and the demands of his faith are so "inward," that he is unaware of any contradiction between the world's means and the life of faith. One adopts television or radio without hesitation, without questioning the psychological effects of these devices, or the validity of the witness borne through these media. Such concerns carry little weight where there is assurance of efficiency and utility.

This Christian who brings the world into the Church is also a man who, like everyone else, is up-to-the-minute. He has undergone that bias typical of modern man (we shall deal with it later in connection with politics) which, in the Church as well, causes him to be interested only in the latest news. Moreover, he forgets it as soon as something else comes along. In any case, in consequence of this up-to-the-minute attitude, he no longer exhibits any interest in the eternal, in that which endures, in the reading of the Bible, which at least we must by all means apply to "present-day problems," otherwise he cannot see what good it is.

This passion for the latest thing leads the member conformed to the world to confine his interests solely to the problems of the world. A century ago Protestants could be accused of being interested only in the soul and in the interior life. That was, to be sure, an error, but the bias of our own day is no less an error. Our interest is confined to economic and social problems, *such as the world defines them, sees them and chooses to present them.*

This last point is the heart of the matter. We put on the world's glasses in order to see only what the world sees. The Christian is characterized by the fact that he perceives problems *when* the world perceives them, and *as* it states them. He exhibits no clarity of vision which would permit him to see sooner, more deeply, or further. In my opinion, it is not a matter of intelligence, but of the Holy Spirit. One need only read Protestant newspapers and magazines to realize that they contain, six months later, exactly the same treatment of hunger, overpopulation, decolonization, unionism and mass culture that one can read anywhere. Eighty percent of their articles have to do with social and political problems, stated in exactly the same terms in which the world states them.

But if Christians thus limit themselves to a mere ratification of the world's decisions, and of its self-diagnosis; if they perceive problems when and as non-Christians claim to state them; if they associate themselves without reservation with non-Christian activities, then, of course, the way is paved for an easy contact with others. Christians, in that case, are bringing to people just what the latter expect of religion. But precisely at that moment the Christian transforms the revealed truth into a religion. He uses it to supply the wants of man and to satisfy the human heart. That, more than philosophic error, is the real transition from revelation to religion.

At the same time it represents a dreadful confusion between the apostolate and conformity. Haven't we seen it maintained recently that preaching should take as its point of departure not the biblical text but the world's problems as people see them? There is nothing new or original about that. I have heard sermons on the virtue of work and on the value of western civilization. It is not true that one can take these problems as the "point of departure" for preaching the Gospel. If the Gospel is the overflowing of grace there is no unbroken continuity, and if the preaching is faithful the break will be as noticeable as if one simply used the written word as the point of departure. The apostolate is in no way commensurate with positions taken on the world's problems as the world sees them. The latter, at most, can only give rise to false opportunities, pseudo-encounters and numerous misunderstandings. It is essential to grasp the extent to which this principle of taking as one's point of departure the problems posed by non-Christians after they have become certain, obvious and grievous for all (even when they come through fallacious news coverage and in consequence of propaganda efforts) leads to a fundamental modification of the faith and of revelation.

We have just said that such a principle involves a transformation in religion. Let's be specific: The moment Christians make it a habit to understand questions which the world has elaborated, they adopt at the same time a certain number of ideological positions, responses and doctrines which also originate in the world. It can hardly be otherwise the moment one confines oneself to the basic notions of the problem as defined by non-Christians. In so doing, Christians achieve an exact confirmation of the analysis of Marx, according to which Christianity is a superstructure. When one takes world hunger as *the problem* par excellence and repeats the analyses of Castro and others, when he progressively adapts Christianity to those views, and when preaching latches on to that—then Marx is right!

This Christianity is a religion which develops in terms of the world's economic and technological evolution, and whose aim is to provide ideological and moral satisfactions to those who are in fact *incapable* of changing the situation. It is a substitute. If it be said that Christianity should *arouse* people to action in changing the situation, then those who enter that work-area find out very soon how useless, futile and ineffective Christianity is in all that. Further, since the Christian is involved in a gigantic, technical and "weighty" endeavor, he soon discards spiritual preoccupations and the pursuit of faith, for these are now mere embarrassments and epiphenomena.

Marx's scheme is accurate regarding a Christianity which is simply the ideology of the world. That was the case with the bourgeois Christianity of the nineteenth century. It is also the case with Christianity "on fire with the world's problems." To seize upon problems *as the world states them,* to accept the world's basic notions of them, its self-sufficient prescriptions for a solution, and to give them first place, is to become part of the dialectical trend as Karl Marx described it. This is accurate to the very extent to which Christians allow themselves to be confined, that is to say, to the extent to which they cease to represent the Wholly Other who intervenes and who reintroduces miracle into history.

Now in acting thus, Christians are abandoning the very thing which is their function with respect to the world, and which has a bearing on the course of events in this century. That function is to introduce a tension, an element of contradiction and conflict, which replaces the false dialectic of Marx with a true dialectic. However, this true dialectic cannot exist in the concrete situations of the world unless Christians really have another fatherland and are "ambassadors" for Christ, "strangers" among the nations and "exiles" on the earth. If they are not that, they can keep on declaring that Christ is Lord, but they still limit themselves to confirming the course of the world as it is.

They are of no real use to the people of these times. They are only worth something insofar as they place themselves in dialectical tension with the world. They are only useful to the degree in which they *reject* the problem within which the world thinks to enclose itself when dealing with concrete economic and social situations. Their function in such situations is to find new and different principles which are true, new and different proposals resulting from this other way of stating a question.

Failure to fulfill that function involves much more than merely accepting a statement about a social, political or economic affair such as the newspapers and essayists present it to us. It is necessarily to adopt the criteria in terms of which the statement was put together.

Every social body has its criteria of the good, of the validity of life, of the meaning of action, etc. For those who belong to that social body such criteria are not at all objects of thought.* They are axiomatic and beyond dispute. They go without saying. Whoever

---

* Obviously, the philosophers are not the ones who produce them. We are not talking about ideas or philosophies, but about what we have treated elsewhere as collective and sociological presuppositions.

questions them puts himself outside the society. They
are the terms in which everything is seen, considered
and judged.

One of our criteria of the good, for example, is the increase in the standard of living. Only when one has a
sufficiently high standard of living can one lead a
"human life worthy of the name." Thanks to the raising
of the standard of living, cultural and intellectual, and
even moral and spiritual development become possible.
That is one of those obvious things.* I find that all
Christians accept this without taking note of the fact
that it is purely and simply an ideological concept dat-
ing from the nineteenth century which went along with
a substantial increase in the standard of living. It is not
an obvious truth for all time and for humanity as a
whole. There have always been groups, in fact, with
other criteria. Thus, in the Roman world of the first
century the accepted idea, the commonplace, the axiom
believed by all, was clearly that of the value of order
and unity. Everything was done to that end. Everything
was judged in relation to that order and to that unity.†

Now, do we see Christian circles adopting those criteria? It would appear that Jesus and his disciples were
entirely indifferent to that kind of thinking. In Paul,
and in the Acts of the Apostles, there is not a shadow of
an allusion to notions with which we have become familiar. These are later introduced into Christian
thought by persons won over to the Roman ideology.

* I attempt, in *The Technological Society,* to show that this belief is
incorrect.

† Not only by the Roman administrators, for private letters and records
of the Hellenic milieu preserved in papyri show this to be true also for
non-Romans and for private individuals.

For example: Thanks to the system of roads, thanks to safety at sea, thanks to good transportation made possible by the Roman order, the Gospel was able to be spread abroad, *therefore* this work of Rome is greatly to be commended, and the criterion of order accepted in the Empire is valid (but the modern conclusion has also been drawn, that Christianity *only existed* thanks to Roman order!). Or again: Thanks to the Roman conquest, thanks to the unification of the Mediterranean world under the authority of the Caesars, thanks to the unity of the Empire, the adoption of Christianity was made possible for all (it is noteworthy that this was never mentioned in Holy Scripture as a reason for loyalty to Caesar!), *therefore* unity is a criterion of great importance!

That was, in fact, set forth during the reigns of Constantine and Justinian, and again even more strongly by Charlemagne. At that time the unity of the Empire meant the possibility, and even the guarantee, of the unity of the faith. It was even a stage in the journey toward the Heavenly Jerusalem. The unification of the world under the authority of the Christian Caesar was progress toward unification in the hands of the Lord.*

We who no longer share those collective presuppositions, and who have witnessed the *result* of such adulteration, can easily discern the errors of that attitude. Yet we repeat exactly the same error. We adopt just the same attitude and embrace, in fact, the same heresy with regard to the presuppositions of our own

* Turning things upside down, non-Christian philosophers of history have found it possible to use the same premise to explain that it was the universalism of the Empire which had been the cause of Christian universalism.

time. To say that the faith should develop, that evangelization should become possible as a result of an increase
in the standard of living, or that the latter is the normal
expression of charity, is to say the same thing the Christians of the fourth to the tenth centuries said about
order and universalism!

Today we have a different premise from which to
start, but one which is likewise dictated by the powers
of the world. Speaking of heresy, we witness, for example, that of Teilhard de Chardin basing itself precisely
on the collective and sociological presuppositions of our
society. It is telling us that in adopting the present
course of the world (technology, socialization, population increase) we are right in line with the preparation
of the Kingdom of God, and that this universalism is
leading us toward the great leap into the omega point.
We are indeed coming back to the same idea as that of
Charlemagne, only starting from a different ideology
supplied by the world!

ADAPTING CHRISTIANITY TO THE
WORLD'S THINKING

The foregoing exposition causes us to observe that a
great many of our attitudes and principles which we
adopt as Christian are nothing but products of our
subjection to the world. But that subjection also leads
us to a conscious or unconscious adaptation of our
thinking to the world's thinking. How often have we
heard it said, for example, that to affirm this or that
item in the Bible is merely to recall an outmoded civilization. Those biblical statements are not part of the
Christian message. They were the human involvement

which Paul, and even Jesus, shared with their society. We are taking values of an earlier civilization, which have since been done away with, and are attaching them to Christianity, even making them a part of Christianity itself. We should, to the contrary, stick to the inner kernel of the Gospel and revive it in terms of the coming world and its values.

To this contention, which has become classic today, I pose three objections. First of all, I have found no one, so far, who is able to draw a clear line (apart from vague and nebulous generalizations) between what is supposed to be the much-touted inviolable kernel and that which comes from the surrounding civilization. It is the same attempt, on other grounds, as that by which historians of the nineteenth century hoped to use textual criticism finally to uncover the "actual" words of Jesus Christ and to put them beyond scientific dispute. That effort turned out to be completely futile, as one of the great practitioners of the science acknowledged toward the end of his life. On the theological level, the claim to distinguish in Jesus Christ what is of God and what is of man represents the same sort of futility.

In the second place, no one has demonstrated that those values which one rejects—those ethical instructions, that social view, that anthropology—were *only* assumptions of a bygone civilization. After all, even if they are *also* to be credited to a form of traditional civilization, it is quite possible that they were *nevertheless* what God willed for man in the order of the fall, or in obedience to his will. Similarly, the fact that other religions of the Mediterranean basin speak of resurrection with Atys, or with Osiris, is no reason for our simply saying that the resurrection of Jesus Christ is the same thing. The fact that property and inheritance existed in the Mediterranean world does not justify us in declaring that what the Bible says about those things is totally superseded! One would have to be able to show that it is not *also* the will of God.

In taking such an attitude, one is not facing seriously the question of the validity of a given biblical statement about man or society in dependence upon and in relation to Jesus Christ. Conversely, one is not facing seriously the question of the validity of the values of modern society (or of that of tomorrow) to which Christianity is supposed to be adapted. One refuses to judge those values (we shall see why). They are accepted because they exist, and one is afraid of playing the role of the judges of Galilee all over again! But we need, at least, to ask ourselves: "What if it were not merely a matter of form, of adopting earlier concepts, when the Bible speaks to us (differently from the way the world does) of money, of work, of technology, of the big city? And what if it was not by a mere historical accident that the Bible reveals to us values other than those proclaimed by our society?" But we are careful not to ask those questions.

Finally, the basis for all this talk about the need to rethink Christianity in terms of today's society is, in the last analysis, a version of one of the world's dominant ideas, the idea of adjustment! The Americans make it a key word in social life, and Mao says the same thing with his business of "the mold." The important thing, above all else, is to adapt oneself to the world. One must take a positive attitude, an open, acquiescent and extroverted attitude. The attitude of refusal is very much looked down upon as a symptom of complexes and of immaturity. The unadjusted person is unanimously spurned by psychologists and sociologists. We have reference to innumerable works of social psychology. Society appears so obviously excellent that people should, *above all,* adjust to it. That is the point of departure without which nothing is possible. The slogan of adjustment is strictly unanimous, and Christians have not escaped it. Before facing any other question, one must be "a person of our time." We have read that and heard it a hundred times from Christians also.

Now this idea of adapting ourselves to the world around us is definitely not a biblical teaching, but a watchword of the world. Let us remember, once again, that we are not preaching a systematic maladjustment, but that we simply are rejecting any value whatever of adaptation to the world, that we consider it a betrayal to justify such adaptation on the ground of "Christian motivations," and again that it is a betrayal to pretend to adapt our faith, our theological thinking, our Christian life, to this world. In adapting, one imports into the faith the *"stoikeia,"* the rudiments of the world, against which we are expressly warned.*

The watchword of adjustment is linked with the belief in progress. Here again we are confronted with a modern myth, which has no basis in scripture. It is well known where this myth and this collective faith in progress come from, and what they feed on. We know very well that it is a matter of an explicitly anti-Christian philosophy, that it is a matter of a blind admiration for the successes of science and technology, that it represents a powerful political trend, and that it is an axio-

---

* Galatians 4:3, 9; Colossians 2:8, 20.

matic belief common to all. Under these conditions, the
Christian, since he is a man of this world, offers no resistance to the enthusiasm. He, too, wants to share in
the progress.

That leads us, then, to point out one of the sentiments which is very frequent among Christians: the
fear of being shunted to one side in the human adventure, the fear of being on the bank while the stream of
history flows by, the fear of not being part of the action,
the fear of not being among the leaders of progress and
of the future, the fear of missing out on something important which mankind is about to bring off! All
around us there are people who are doing great things,
are engaged in demonstrably useful works. *They* are the
ones who are building the future. And we? We Christians are looked upon as poor fools, stuck with idle and
outmoded beliefs. We are thought of as useless and
weak. They tell us we are victims of a slave morality
(Hitler), or of a bourgeois morality (the communists).
They inform us that we are about to disappear, automatically, in consequence of the progress of science or
of the course of history.

And indeed it is true. If we refuse to run with everybody else, we shall be left behind. That seems undeni-
able. So let's run and work like everybody else to build
that same future! Then we'll have the feeling of being
good for something. Then we shall avoid those deroga-
tory judgments against Christians and Christianity.

One gets out of it as best one can. For example, a distinction can be made between "two values," "two salva-
tions." One is historic, temporal, the object of progress;
the other is eternal, the object of revelation. It is also
possible to distinguish different levels on which prog-

ress is made, etc. In any case it is a matter of reincor-
porating progress into some expression of Christian
thought, and so to show that Christians are not out of
the running.

Of course one cannot, even so, avoid stumbling over
the eschatological event, but one stays ahead by accus-
ing of dark prophecy, gloomy thoughts and a taste for
tragedy and apocalyptic catastrophe, all those who remind us, whether we like it or not, of the limit which
revelation sets on the history of man, on his "progress,"
on the development of his civilization, and that it is the
judgment of Babylon which brings about its annihilation.

The assumption of man's work in the Heavenly Jerusalem, by the grace of God, has nothing to do with
progress. The criticisms leveled at those who remind us
of this clear principle of scripture have the character of
labels rather than arguments. They do not alter the content of revelation in the least. What does alter it is the
attempt to adapt the theology and teaching given to the
faithful to ideas like that of progress.

We have numerous examples of these "attempt-
temptations." Thus, for a given Christian, to "bear witness" no longer means to proclaim the Lord, but to participate in political meetings and to post the placards of
a political party (which have strictly no connection
with preaching the Gospel). This is a genuine fact. Similarly, from the pen and from the mouth of numerous
authorities in the Church, we have this assertion: "It's a
fact. It isn't for us to ask whether it is good or bad. That
is a useless question." Technology? It's a fact. To
"judge" it would be useless (this was a reply made by a
theologian in a National Synod). Freedom of women?

It's a fact. It is useless to "judge" it (this was declared by a leader of "Young Women" movements). Communism? It's a fact (a statement made during a debate on communism in the National Synod). Mass culture? There's no need to argue about its value. It has *a* value, that of existing, etc.

Yet, if one thus attributes inherent value to fact, and if the moment the fact exists it is useless to bring an ethical or spiritual judgment to bear upon it, then I say that this should be carried to its logical conclusion. Capitalism? It's a fact. War? It's a fact. Parachutists? It's a fact. Torture? That's a gross fact. And the police? If you think to choose among these facts, and you tell me that the fact "emancipation of women" should be accepted, but not "torture," then I sense that there is some reason for that choice and that, when all is said and done, you agree with the first but you disagree with the second. Therefore you have made a moral choice, and one is quite simply hypocritical and dishonest in advancing the argument that one is faced with a fact, and that moral judgment is to be avoided on that account.

There remains, moreover, the question why one employs that argument. The answer, alas, is easy. In reality, one would be hard put to it to find the biblical and theological bases which would bring us closer to loyal consent, so one avoids debate by eliminating the moral problem on the ground that facts elude such judgment (which already seems to me very suspect theologically!). But especially is it a matter of rhetoric when one employs it on behalf of what is actually one of the absolute values of our world. A fact is a final value. One yields to the fact. Nothing can be done about it. Whenever, in an ordinary argument, one person is able to say

to the other: "First of all, it's a fact," there is nothing to
be said in reply.

To give up passing judgment on a fact, to assume
that all one can do from then on is to yield to it, to adjust to it, that is precisely and totally to abandon the
Christian life in its entirety. There is no position more
radically anti-Christian than to give way to a fact. It is
to accept fate. It is to agree that the material factor is
the determining one. It is to agree that the Christian
life is nothing but a morality. At the same time, it is a
renunciation of spiritual discernment, and of the possibility of injecting truth into the context of reality.

That entails enormous consequences, which, to be
sure, are never foreseen by those Christians who think
they are realists because they announce: "It's a fact."
For example, every government established by force becomes legitimate because it exists. That is indeed the
actual judgment of the world. Can it be the Christian
judgment?

Christians obey the world's logical inconsistencies.
Their thinking is so unstable that the very ones who accept fact as final judgment in matters of technology,
progress, mass culture, economic growth, urbanization,
etc., are the same ones who reject fact in the case of
colonialism or of the present government. But perhaps,
again, this is nothing but a conformism, because they
are rejecting colonialism after it has been defeated and
is disappearing, and capitalism after the great majority
are condemning it, and when the structure of society is
moving in the direction of socialism.

Once again, let's make it clear that it is no part of our
thinking to deny the facts, or to say that they do not
have to be taken into account. What we are saying is

simply that it is a gross intellectual error to transform fact into a *value,* to conceive of fact as being or as containing a value in and of itself. We are saying that it is a gross moral error to renounce judging a fact, that it is a gross spiritual error to urge man to bow before fact, that is to say, before the *fatality* of whatever exists. If the argument is frequently employed in Christian circles, it is simply because one knows that the Christian participant in a dialogue will, as a man of this world, be immediately convinced by that type of reasoning before which the whole world bows.

Again, that same kind of adaptation leads to a change in the concept of love of neighbor. The traditional idea was that this love had to do with a person of one's acquaintance, to whom one was close, and that love would only take place in the proximity of person to person. Yes, but how times have changed! On the one hand, there is the vastness of the interrelationships created by the technological media, the telephone, newspapers, the radio. There are contacts at a distance, thanks to speed of communication. On the other hand, there is a collective mutuality of interests which has become worldwide. Every event throughout the world has its repercussions on all, and we can no longer remain indifferent, for we are subjected to the aftereffects of economic and political decisions the world over. Conversely, our decisions have their repercussions on everybody else. When the Suez was attacked by France and England, the whole of Asia and Africa felt it and reacted. Henceforth our lives are truly bound up with the lives of all.

Furthermore, the same result is produced by the spread of democratic structures. *Individuals* in all nations are more and more affected, but they also feel

more and more accountable. Now the present-day
Christian feels that he should shoulder his part of this
collectivity of interests, which exists in actuality, and
that he should turn it into the expression of a higher
value. Since he is a Christian, he thinks to transform
simple, sociological obedience, and the purely natural
responses, into a spiritual obedience and a virtue. He
will explain that if he wishes to participate in the larger
works of man it is for theological reasons, and that if he
shares the popular emotions and political fears, that is
because he has a lively sense of the community in which
God has placed him. He wants to assume his responsibilities.

Here I'm afraid it is necessary to be somewhat cruel,
and to say that if the Christian performs the same works
as all the world, if he has the same hopes and fears as everybody else, it is for the same reasons, the reasons of
the milieu. It is because he is conditioned by the socio-
economic factor.

But it is also true that the Christian experiences a
quite lively sentiment of community and of collectivity.
However, that is not peculiar to him. It is surely one of
the factors of conformity to the world, since ninety-nine
percent of the members of society, in one way or another, put the value of the community, of the group, of
the society in the forefront. This is true whether we are
thinking of social psychologists, or philosophers in the
wake of Teilhard de Chardin, or *Marie-Claire* instruct-
ing women how to become part of the community, or
sportsmen extolling team sports, etc. In any case, the
Christian shares this sentiment, and feels himself one
with the whole of mankind.

He definitely no longer sees himself as "a people

apart," "a holy nation." He wants to be a man among men. Sometimes one comes to the point of demanding of God: "Either save all of us, all humanity from the beginning to the end, without any exceptions, or else we Christians refuse to be saved if we are to be saved alone." This attitude, which only Jesus Christ can assume before God, represents, I know, the profound sentiment of a great many Christians who dare not put it that crudely (and here once more we have an attitude, which we come upon again and again, in which the Christian puts himself in the place of Jesus Christ or of God).

The Christian of our day is a person who has taken man's part (and that is very good!) *instead of* (and this is very bad!) God's part in the midst of men. It is the opposite of that which we reproach many of our forbears for having done, having taken God's part exclusively, to the point of forsaking or scorning man. (Let's not reason from the fact that *God* took man's part and went over to his side, because he is God!) But here we are led still further toward a transformation of the concept of love of neighbor.

The theory of "distant relationships" and of the extension of love is sufficiently important to warrant our stopping over it briefly. Essentially it amounts to considering love as a dimension which covers the whole of creation, including man and his works, and which is to be seen obviously in the lordship of Jesus Christ. It rejects the antinomy between one's neighbor, the individual nearby, and a copartner, that is to say, the person with whom I have only societal relations, to whom I am bound solely by sociological ties. Finally, we must realize that charity has import for a social institution as well as for a personal encounter. Hence love is applicable both to institutions and to collective man, with whom I enter into relationship through the media of mass communication, and by means of the airplane or the telephone, and political activity is the expression of this love at a distance.

There must be obvious agreement with this when it is a question of denouncing the shrunken view of charity in the bourgeois outlook, and of reminding ourselves that personal relationship should not be an escape, but that "sometimes it operates through the copartner relationship, sometimes it is worked out on the fringe of that relationship, and sometimes it opposes it." We can readily agree in denouncing an eschatology —usually set up a little too simplistically in order to demolish it more easily—which condemns the world of the copartner in order to retreat into the dream of small prophetic communities. Finally, we need to remember that the neighbor relationship is not superior for being "natural," nor are other relationships inferior because not in conformity with nature.

These things granted, and they are no more than truisms, it seems to us that the theory of distant relationships is quite heretical and anti-biblical. Its point of departure is already significant, namely, that we are living in a society which is no longer based on direct personal relationships, but on media and on distant and complex collective interests. Technological progress and democratic advances put us in contact with all. How can we manage to incorporate that into Christianity? How are we to think of Christianity in terms of this factual situation? (I contend that this is a false question.)

What is more, we are rediscovering the validity of history, since interpersonal relations are not historical. They are historically marginal and insufficient.

With that beginning, the revelation concerning love is altered. That is why I say that a false question is being asked. It is a question *natural* to the intellect of man, but *false* in as far as it *falsifies* revelation.

From that point on, we witness successive lapses of language. One slips verbally from administrative officials to the State. One slips from love to social and economic service. One slips from active charity to "what makes sense." One slips from a command given to each of us to the meaning of the lordship of God over history. One slips from the normal course of friendship by mail or telephone to love of neighbor, etc. All these unconscious lapses, no one of which is serious in itself, add up to a complete reversal of the situation, after having rendered it quite obscure.

But two results are clear. The first is abstraction. All biblical instruction is shifted by a mechanism of abstraction (thus, administrative officials to the institution or the State, etc. We must remember that this abstraction existed in Paul's time also, and it is characteristic of him that he personalizes everything, instead of leaving it in the abstract language of the jurists of his time!). It is a case of "abstract love," and as a matter of fact one cannot get by otherwise if it is a question of bringing global social relations within the framework of love. In the second place, we are led to putting ourselves in the place of God. That God loves all men, that God's love is expressed in his lordship over history, that God becomes the neighbor of every copartner, so much we know. But he is God, and what is being proposed to us in this theory is that we put ourselves on his level.

Over against that, let us recall some simple rudiments. The commandment which is given us is very clear. It does not have to do with the historic dimension, nor with mankind, nor even with neighbors, but with a single person, your neighbor. The explanation is also simple. Jesus shows how the good Samaritan transformed the relationship with a copartner (Samaritan—Jew, which *is not* a love relationship, and which love neither covers nor touches) into a relationship with a neighbor, exclusive of all others.

Love

Every act of love shown in scripture involves causing a person to *come out* of his status of anonymity, derived from collectivity, the crowd, etc., in order, through a purely personal relationship, to transform him into a person known and distinguished by his name. Love, biblically, is never turned into something for media, nor is it collectivized, abstract or general. Furthermore, the new social conditions are no reason for altering the revelation concerning love. That revelation is an express impugning of all abstraction. Love exercised through distant relationship is simple hypocrisy, because it goes beyond the human possibilities, and it is an idealism which avoids the reality of the love shown forth in scripture. Technological means and population increase can create mechanized communities of interest, doing away with personal encounter through the multiplicity of external contacts and through the formation of "the solitary crowd." It is dreadful to confuse a "public service" with the service of love.

It is false to say that charity seldom appears except

when I touch a common condition in the other person which takes the form of a collective misfortune: the wage-earning class, colonial exploitation, etc. The reverse is true biblically. As long as I am concentrating on this collective misfortune I am at the level of political revolt, institutional reform, etc., but that precisely is not charity. The latter takes place when the collective misfortune becomes so personalized in this neighbor that it fades out as "collective" and as "status," in order to leave only the bleeding flesh and soul. It is the human being, not his status as member of a group, that is in the category of charity. (I know that in saying that, I am running counter to modern theories on the human being and social class. I simply believe them incorrect, and that will appear soon.) Jesus also had to do with collective misfortune and group status. He showed, both in the story of the Samaritan and in that of the massacred Galileans, that it was a matter of clearing these away in favor of another reality. To speak of distant relationships in charity is to go against the very movement itself of charity as described for us in the Bible, where the person-to-person relationship is its distinguishing characteristic.

Finally, we must not forget that, in revealing to us what love is, Christ precisely did not come as *Pantocrator,* but as Jesus, that is to say, localized. He addressed himself to a very small number of persons, with whom he established personal relations, and he moved *away from* their socio-political culture.

In a civilization which tends to exclude "agape" and to replace it, either with justice, or with "eros," or with the group, the Christian presence in the world consists specifically in maintaining agape, and in not confusing it with other things. What, in truth, the person of our day can find most helpful is a break in his loneliness, in his psychological misery, through agape. That is much more important than political action. To claim to lead Christians into political activity as an extension of love on a worldwide scale is to deny to love its own special expression displayed to us in the Bible. It is to rob the Christian presence in the world of its true usefulness.

This concern for "the world" as object of the Christian's love has become so great today that in the end we encounter a determination to bear responsibility for the totality of suffering. We encounter the pretense of taking upon oneself the misery of the whole world, that of tortured Algerians, that of the inhabitants of India who are dying of hunger, and that of the Tibetans crushed and oppressed by the Chinese.*

Now scripture never asks us to bear the world's suffering. It is enough to bear that of one's neighbor. Once again, we encounter the very bad presumption of putting ourselves in the place of Jesus Christ, who alone bears the sufferings of the Algerians, the Tibetans and the inhabitants of India. He does not ask us to substitute ourselves for him.

That does not mean that we are to be indifferent to the sufferings of mankind! But it does mean that my only actual concern is the one which is near enough to me, and close enough to my size, so that I might *really*

---

* In this case, it is I who add this, for in truth the Tibetans, although horribly ill-fated, much more so than the Algerians, do not interest our Protestants too much! Neither do the Jews of Morocco, nor the Catholics and intellectuals of Cuba, nor the Puerto Ricans in the United States, nor the Hungarians crushed by the Russians, etc. What we have here is a bad conscience which is selective (we shall meet up with it again).

do something about it. Revelation, in its rigorous realism, does not ask us to torture ourselves over universal ideas and information, nor to lose sleep over news items from everywhere. As Paul says so well: "For if the readiness is there, it is acceptable according to what a man has, not according to what he has not" (2 Corinthians 8:12).

Especially should we not put on an act, as a bad conscience often incites us to do. We should not suppose that we have taken action on the world's suffering because we have signed a petition on behalf of the Hungarians or the Algerians, or because we have demonstrated in the streets, or have given the price of a meal to alleviate world famine. Those are evil little substitutes for grace. They are the not-too-innocent ploys of the devil.

* * *

3

The Sociological Examination
of Conscience

I do not in the least dispute the validity of certain scientific findings. I feel that, as Christians, we need to accept
them and use them. It seems to me necessary, for example, to bring the life of the Church face to face with certain (very pertinent!) conclusions of sociology and of
social psychology. We have to accept what I would call
the *critical function* of sociology in relation to the
Church, just as we have to accept historical criticism.
What I have been saying above is in no way a contradiction of that principle, provided we do not treat scientific conclusions as absolutes.

It is not a matter of religious sociology, which is
futile and academic when it confines itself to counting
Easter communions, reckoning the percentage of faithful within an ecclesiastical boundary, or doing research

on the social backgrounds of the clergy! Insofar as the Church is a group made up of people, it is a sociological entity. As such it is subject to the same tendencies as all other sociological bodies. For a non-Christian, that is all it is. Hence no problem is posed. For a Christian, it is *first of all* the body of Christ, but it is also the human group.

The questions raised by sociology, then, are: To what degree does the Church behave purely and simply as a sociological body? To what degree is it an expression of *something else* which is not dependent on sociology: the presence on earth of the Kingdom of Heaven, the action of the Holy Spirit? To what degree is its faith in the Lord an expression of something unique among human groups? That uniqueness cannot be seen from the outside. There are no obvious signs, significant in themselves, which would strike a non-Christian. (However: "See how they love one another!" Perhaps that is, in effect, the one non-sociological, human mark of distinction which might be visible—the love *among* Christians.) But, in any case, those inside should ask this question of themselves, should let the question be asked, should submit to being questioned about it, for it is a dreadfully painful matter. I have not yielded to any other viewpoint in chapters 1 and 2.

Sociology, rigorously applied, strips the Church of a large portion of what we think of as her distinctive marks, works of faith, expressions of truth. We must submit to the difficult consideration of this situation. It is an awakening to what we really are, and an unmasking of our cleverness. It is a case of humility which strips us naked (for, in spite of everything, the faith remains firmly based on the Word of God), which causes us to invest the Lord with everything which has been taken away from us.

This surgical operation need not discourage us, nor call in question the revelation or our faith, but it should make us marvel all the more that there is a Church. It should help us to understand all the more that everything depends on the free decision of God's love, and to give glory to God that the Prince of this world does not control us more than he does!

Let us go still further down this painful road. Youth polls show that practically the same proportion of young people belong to youth movements, whether they are Christians or not. Similarly, "conscious, deliberate Christians," accountable as active members of our churches, represent a percentage of the total member-ship (10%) equivalent to that in any other group whatsoever. When questionnaires on a given problem in the life of the Church are sent out to Church mem-bers, the proportion who reply is the same as for busi-ness or political questionnaires. The behavior of Chris-tians as a group, in many important spheres, is the same as that of non-Christians (sexual behavior, for example, as seen in the Kinsey Report). When there is a public conference on evangelism, organized with all the mod-ern means, one obtains the same percentages of persons interested, or of persons directly involved, as for a polit-ical conference, or for one on the culture, or on alcohol-ism. So we are obliged to conclude that propaganda methods are at work, and not the Holy Spirit.

We find in the Church, as in ancient groups, the same continuity of culture and tradition, in the same forms and with the same percentages. Ninety percent of the Church is made up of persons drawn from an earlier

Protestant family background, just as in political groups or social classes. This also seems to rule out independent conversion by the Holy Spirit. It would be surprising indeed if the Holy Spirit manifested himself in a specific culture and if, in effect, there were a sort of hereditary transmission. Alas, we must acknowledge, to the contrary, that what we have here is a sociological continuity.

Note, likewise, that the famous "crisis," in the course of which young people disappear from the Church after their catechetical instruction at age 17, only to reappear (at least a certain number of them) at age 25, is a quite classic phenomenon in other groups. It is a crisis of flight from the adult world, just at the time when it is indispensable that one become part of it, a crisis of protest against all that was given to the young person during childhood, etc. It is not unique behavior but very habitual, and one which takes place in the same proportions elsewhere.

Finally, let us observe that the Protestant Church exhibits reactions typical of minority groups of whatever kind (greater solidarity, a tendency to go to political extremes, payment of higher contributions than is the case with majority groups, a multiplicity of newspapers, etc.). These are purely sociological reactions.

We are obliged to go still further. Is there not a sociological influence to be seen in certain theological choices, in certain viewpoints, in certain silences? One very characteristic aspect is the objection to ethics. A concern to avoid anything which might hurt non-Christians, to avoid alienating them by ethical requirements, the anxiety to resolve tensions and conflicts.

Such fears make us less and less uncompromising in the sphere of ethics. We admit, for example, that to maintain tensions and conflicts is an "adolescent" attitude, and so we give in to the collective judgment of society. We think it the part of charity to resolve tensions and conflicts (a typical application of the new sociological line)! Yet every moral imperative creates tensions, so from now on we are prepared to give up requirements in favor of easier relations.

Morality tends to retreat into the background, not only for theological reasons (which are true but I dare say, *in this case,* secondary), but also because we are living in a culture in which morality is condemned from all sides as being a requirement, a facing-up to a specific "Yes" or a specific "No," a standing for a mode of conduct which is hard. We dare not place ourselves, and still less others, in confrontation with an explicit commandment which envisages the adoption of a peculiar attitude.

Besides, "Christian" ethics seems definitely bound up with "bourgeois morality." It seems, in fact, to be a mere reflection of the same. That leaves two possibilities: Either it is a morality which goes without saying, which is axiomatic in the bourgeois culture, in which case it is in no sense the presence of the impossible will of God for us; or else it is no longer accepted or listened to in the anti-bourgeois, intellectual or workers' circles. So it is a purely sociological reaction, having nothing to do with a deeper ethical understanding, or with a higher level of requirement.

In order, then, to avoid coming forth with clear and specific ethical requirements, the tendency is to retreat into a theology of transcendence, from which it is very

difficult to formulate a clear ethical statement. The re-
formers already experienced that great difficulty, which
led, by reaction, to Protestant moralism. As a matter of
fact, we face the same difficulty with the theology of
Karl Barth, but we are not waylaid into moralism because of our submission to the surrounding culture,
which is completely immoral, or antimoral. Only we
need to recognize that our scorn for the law, our rejection of morality, our criticism of bourgeois morality, do
not come from the glorious liberty of the children of
God, but from our swimming with the world's current.

If it be said that my critique is guesswork, and that I
really know nothing about it, I reply that there is a very
sure test. We are forced by theology (which I think is a
good one!) into declaring for innovation, for personal
and free decision in the domain of commitment, and for
the personalizing of attitudes, in terms of a faith which
receives God's commandment as Gospel. But where, in
the Christian circles with which I am acquainted, do I
see this innovation, this decision, this freedom, this personalizing? I see people, like myself, who conduct themselves exactly like everybody else. This liberty which
comes from faith leads to a pure and simple conformity
to the ways of society. That seems to me odd, to say the
least.

Liberty with regard to "the law" does not have us
going infinitely beyond the requirements of the law, as
Jesus Christ strictly specified. It is rather a pretext for
staying infinitely this side of that, for falling short even
of that which the law requires, in other words, for remaining at the popular level. To be sure, strict Sunday
observance is ridiculous, and not in the least in accord
with freedom toward the law! Yet, instead of making

Sunday into an innovation of liberty for the glory and
the adoration of the Lord, and for meditation, Protestants go off to the country in automobiles, just like 72%
of the French (in the springtime)!

Let's get into a still more cruel area, that of theology.
There, too, we have to submit to questioning by the
non-Christian making use of sociology.

What about ecumenism? Is it out of pure loyalty to
the will of Christ, his will to gather together his
Church, that the ecumenical movement is developing?
If it had occurred, let us say, in the seventeenth century,
I would have answered: Yes, without hesitation. But
today? How many subsidiary and sociological motives
can one not uncover! Christianity is everywhere in retreat, disparaged in most of the countries of the world,
overwhelmed by new religions (communism) or by the
spread of old religions (Islam) and by secularism. But
it is the habit of all groups threatened by an external
enemy to merge, and to suppress internal divisions. National unity in time of war is in the same category!

Also, we are witnessing in the contemporary world an
overall trend toward a certain universalism, toward the
formation of racial and political blocs: the western bloc,
the eastern bloc, the Islamic bloc, the black-African
bloc, the creation of a European union, etc. Are the
churches not following exactly the same movement of
combining into a bloc, like all the large units of the
world?

In addition, if we can rejoice at the quieting down of
theological argument and at the lessening of hostile
prejudice among the denominations, can we really give
the credit to the action of the Holy Spirit leading us to

greater charity toward our separated brothers, or must we allow for a purely sociological evolution, namely, the fact that all ideologies the world over are losing their importance, the fact that people are more and more giving up ideological rigidity (e.g., the ambivalence of the leftists), as well as the fact that theological positions no longer interest the public, which nowhere, these days, is aroused en masse by a discussion of the statement of truth? Is it not because we are no longer supported by a popular movement, and because we are won over by the general scepticism toward doctrines and ideologies, that we acknowledge the relative character of our theological positions and, reciprocally, the validity of others?

I do not mean that that is the *only* reason for the ecumenical movement. I mean only to warn against too facile an evaluation as progress toward truth of what is, in part, nothing more than a sociological development. I am familiar with the argument that this world trend can *also* be an act of Providence, and that its worldwide emergence may only be coming to pass for the sake of the unity of the Church. It is similar to the argument that the Roman Empire was *only* for the sake of allowing the Christian faith to develop in the Mediterranean world, or that Christopher Columbus discovered America as part of a mysterious plan of God to have the Gospel taken there (and we know how!). Likewise, in the nineteenth century, imperialism's colonial expansion was also the mysterious plan of God for introducing missions. I am a bit distrustful of these interpretations, and I ask simply that the question be put.

Whenever we witness the emergence and triumph of a theology of transcendence (for, in spite of second reading adjustments, the theology of Karl Barth is still that! And I fully support it), we have to ask ourselves whether it is *only* a more true, more substantial and more inspired statement of revelation (that it *surely* is). It has to be noted that it corresponds to certain assumptions which are human, questionable and embarrassing. It corresponds, in the first place, to the rise in the modern world of trends and doctrines of the irrational. It is interesting that in the nineteenth century the triumph of rationalism sent theologians scurrying in search of a rational theology (from various angles), and that in the twentieth century the outburst of irrationalism in poetry, in painting, in political thought, in psychological interpretation and psychoanalysis, etc., coincides with the same irrationalism in theology.

In the same way, is it not true that the powerful affirmation of the transcendent corresponds to a surrender to the tangible world, to an implicit admission on the part of Christians that they cannot do anything about it (I am not at all suggesting that it is a question of the *spiritual*), and in place of our being able to change the course of the world there is a transfer of our impotence to the all-powerful lordship of God in Jesus Christ? That was the first position of "the Barthians."

But their current desire to be involved in the world is no more convincing, for it corresponds, in the main, to a shift, a rupture, a loss of continuity, between the theological statement and its ethical consequences. On the one hand there is an extremely specific and rigorous statement, and on the other hand, a sort of availability to the world. For example, one can adopt any political stance whatsoever, and travel the ways of the world,

with only a few mental reservations. That is what seems
to us questionable. It is as though, faced with the extreme necessities of the world and finding ourselves
powerless to combat them, we give in to them, all the
while holding in reserve a domain of purity no less extreme, that of theology. It is a facile solution.

For my part, I am convinced that the theology of Karl
Barth should lead to the adoption of very precise positions in the world, specifically with regard to politics,
positions which owe nothing to the laxness we are witnessing, and which are as hard to formulate as to live.
This work has not yet begun.

Lastly, I shall take up the problem of justification.
Sociology teaches us that ideologies are, in great measure, expressions of the concrete conditions of the life of
the group, and that their function is to justify those
conditions in the eyes of the group. Now I am sorry to
observe that in many cases Christians, instead of bringing an element of challenge and criticism to bear on
existing conditions, move in the same direction as the
ideologies.*

If, for example, we examine the content of books, articles and preaching intended for the bourgeois circles
of the Church, we find there mostly the older themes, a
high evaluation of the interior life and of spirituality,
an accent on individual virtue coupled with a refusal to
recognize sociological factors and class affiliation, the

* Also, is it without submitting to sociological pressure that the Church
can declare that "the domain of the State is one of the sectors of the
Church's necessary mission?" Is it not because everybody believes in the
State? And all the articles written by Christians deploring the weakness
and degradation of the State are indeed inspired by the increase, in
fact, of the powers of the State.

showing forth of a liberal good will and an affirmation
of the importance of the orders of creation (property,
family, etc.). We also find an emphasis on the importance of the Church, on church life with its inevitable
tradition, on liturgics and on the perfection of piety,
etc.

If, on the contrary, one turns to the expressions of the
same faith on the part of those who are thrown into the
workers' environment, one finds the accent placed on
justice, on the importance of the poor man, the legiti-
macy of revolt, the exegesis of the prophets in their social significance. One will come upon books on the
"communism of Jesus" (the exact words), and proposals for a workers' Bible (bringing together all the passages on the condemnation of riches and on holding the
poor in high regard. There was a proposal made in
these terms to a National Synod). Communism will be
validated out of love for the poor, and the traditional
Church will be condemned as bourgeois.

Finally, if we look at the expression of the same faith
in intellectual circles, there we find the adoption of the
most current philosophy, support for the "intellectual
socialist" (or liberal socialist?) trend. What is extremely popular in these circles is the necessity for political involvement, the insistence on the community or
team character of all action, a criticism of all morality,
as of all institutions, and "an open attitude toward
world problems" (at least toward those set forth in the
newspapers and magazines of those circles).

Now, in all that the Christian turns Christianity into
a completely ordinary ideology, which functions as the
inner ideology of the group. To be sure, *each* of these
tendencies is *also* true in relation to revelation. It is *also*

an expression of the faith. But the trouble is that this truth and this faith are placed exactly in the context in which they ought not to be placed, exactly at the spot at which they fall under the blow of sociological analysis. That makes it clear that they are turning into errors, because they are turning into ways of conforming to the will of man.

This challenge on the basis of sociological principles is not an attempt to show that the life of the Church is determined by sociological factors, but only to draw the attention of Christians to the fact that it is difficult to separate that which comes from the world and that which is obedience to the Holy Spirit. Consequently, it is incorrect to represent the Church as a body which *ought* to blend with the world. It is at least as important to remember that she should separate herself, should maintain a "distance" with respect to the world. This action does not have preference over the other, but the two actions are interrelated. Before the presence in the world can mean anything, it has to be the presence of "that which is not the world."

If a Church which is a mere association conformed to the propensities of the world, which is informed by the same ideas and prejudices, which follows the same sociological trends, is asked to be present to the world, that means nothing. It is merely a part of the world reuniting with the world. It will neither add nor change anything. Christians are a little too inclined to think that the Church (that preferred part of the Church, of course, with which they agree: The "Fédé" (Federation of Christian Students) for the student, or Taizé, or the Association of Protestant Professionals, or the parish, or a given group, or movement, or work . . .) contains in and by itself the presence of the Wholly Other, the presence of the Lord. Hence this Church need only move in the direction of the world in order to supply the world with what is lacking, the presence of the Lord.

The tendency is the same with regard to Christians as individuals. A man need only declare himself a Christian (and I am not casting doubt on the sincerity of his faith!) and immediately he is expected to provide a Christian presence in a pagan environment. It is supposed to be his duty to take his place on the famous "frontier." But this is forgetting that when Paul was converted he withdrew for years of meditation before beginning his evangelical work. The same was true of Augustine. It is forgetting that the scriptures strictly differentiate the brothers who are "weak," and that one cannot expect everything of everybody. To station the "weak" brother in the most difficult and dangerous post is not necessarily to have confidence in God. It may be to tempt God. It surely is a lack of charity toward the brother, and perhaps it is to lead him into temptation.

To send a young man, full of enthusiasm and confidence in God, into political circles, communist circles *for example,* is to run the risk of destroying him, as we have often observed. For the very reason that neither the thinking nor the behavior of the Christian springs automatically *brand new* from his conversion and faith, for the reason that we have always to take into account the twofold action: You are renewed . . . Be then renewed . . . : we must therefore stress the separation with respect to the world and its thinking.

Especially should we not claim that that goes without saying! What goes without saying is certainly not the new life style of the Christian, nor the renewing of his mind. Alas, what goes without saying is the submission to the world and to the mind of the world, the process of being conformed. The presence in the world supposes, *first of all,* a separation with respect to the world. It is because the Church is *holy* (that is, *separated*) that she is also *sent.* But if the Church is only a non-separated, sociological body (and it isn't enough to say that she is by nature separated because chosen, the body of Christ, bride of the Lord—that is a flight into theological abstraction) neither is she sent, for that sending would be meaningless.

I know the objection that "the Church is only the Church in mission and evangelizing." Yes, of course, but we must not forget the counterpart: the Church as a holy people, as a sacrificing people, as ambassador (that is, belonging to *another* power), as a body (that is, organically *distinct,* different from other bodies and not lost in the indiscriminate mass)!

I also know the objection that "if one waits for the Christian to be *ready* to enter the world, he will never enter it, for he will never be ready." Yes, of course, but there is a difference between a babe in arms and an adult, even though the latter has not yet attained the stature of the fullness of Christ (and never will in this life). What I am saying is that we are sending into the world babes in arms, who are not yet ready for adult tasks, that there is a preparation, both spiritual and intellectual, ethical and sociological, meditative and active, which is *in no way* being given to the Church, nor to those in the Church whom we are urging to become involved in the world.

The fact that they are committed Protestants by background, that they have been confirmed after a sketchy instruction and more or less come to "worship services" —those facts do not make them apt witnesses for Jesus Christ, nor do those experiences insure that their faith will be strengthened (more often it founders) by the encounter with others, nor that they are fulfilling a genuine mission. Already conformed to the world in their thinking and way of life, they will only be conformed a little more by the feeling that they are obeying a vocation. Occasionally the conformity will vary. The son of bourgeois parents, when he becomes a student, will be conformed to the student milieu and will repudiate bourgeois ideas, but that is in no sense a conversion!

When one wakes up to this terrible conformity and to this sociological crushing of the Church, the primary action, the radical decision, is that of separation. The separation is not ultimate, but it is indispensable. When we cite passages which point to the role the people of God have to play among the peoples of the world, we must not forget all those other passages in which the command comes from God: "Separate yourselves . . ." The first order of business is to work at this new way of thinking (which is not at all a matter of the interior life), at this special form of life derived from faith, at this building up of the Church as different from other groups.

If this disengagement does not take place, if this discovery is not made of the specific character of the thought and life of the Christian, then the engagement being recommended to Christians is nothing but the empty pursuit of a fad.

*   *   *

PART TWO

Making the Church Political

4

Clarifying Certain Preliminaries

That our Church today is involved in politics, that it is becoming more and more so, at least in its leading and intellectual circles, appears obvious.* To be convinced of this, one need only read the Church's newspapers and magazines, or follow its synods and assemblies. Yet there is surely quite a distance separating the mass of the faithful in the parishes and certain movements or groups of clergy and intellectuals.

The faithful generally take it for granted that "religion" is a thing apart, that it is wrong to bring politics into the Church. From there they go to the famous distinction (often rightly condemned) between Sunday

* Obviously, in this and the succeeding chapters, we shall have to speak of "politics" without being able to develop and expand many of the points. On this subject we refer the reader to our work: *The Political Illusion*.

and weekdays. The faithful also are involved in politics, but on weekdays only, just as they carry on their businesses, and their faith usually has nothing to do with it. They are citizens on the one hand, and we scarcely dare say that they are "Christians" on the other. The Church's "group leaders," on the contrary, would like to see political issues thrashed out in the Church. They do not want faith separated from reality, and they insist that the political game being played on weekdays be played according to Christian principles.

It goes without saying, and I have written to that effect many times, that I agree in principle with this second outlook. It is unthinkable that the faith should have no effect upon everyday behavior, hence no effect upon politics as well. It is unthinkable that there should be any modern problems which would, in a sense, be the object of a sort of veto and prohibition in the Church. It is unthinkable that the Church should be a snug retreat, into which the world's tumult would never penetrate (and it is all the more unthinkable for being also untrue in reality, as I tried to show in the preceding chapters; and that, in consequence, hypocrisy should be added to theological error).

However, at this point my purpose is not that of determining, on the basis of scripture and theological principle, what the attitude of the Church should be with respect to politics, nor the proper attitude of the Christian toward the State, nor the methods and importance of the Christian's involvement in politics. My purpose is rather to have a look at the factual situation in these matters of the Reformed Church in the year 1962.

EVIDENCES OF POLITICAL INVOLVEMENT

As I have already said, for me it is more a matter of examining the "group leaders." Having indicated that I agree with their governing principles, I am for that very reason forced into a critique in the area of practical application. A consideration of the consequences of the adopted stance seems to me a matter of urgency, not from the standpoint of the opposition (e.g. the purity of the Church and the impurity of politics, the strictly spiritual character of the Church's mission, etc.) but from the standpoint of the theological principles which we hold in common. Now by adopting this stance we make the Church political. Whether or not such a procedure is legitimate, whether or not it is dangerous, is a question we shall look into later on. At this point let us attempt merely to take stock of the fact.

Essentially it is a question of the massive and ever increasing invasion of the Church by political issues. This is not to be confused with the Church-State relationship, because what passes for a political issue in the modern world is much broader than the relationship with the authorities.

If one is looking for signs—the most obvious is the proliferation and use of "position papers." The moment a group of Christians comes together, a synod is called or an assembly meets, they feel compelled to draw up a "political statement." It might be a petition to the government, or an appeal to the people, or a pastoral letter. Over the past fifteen years these "statements" have been counted by the hundreds. They repeat themselves endlessly. They multiply, and sometimes they also contradict themselves! Everyone knows full well that these statements are of no practical use. They are not a way of influencing the government or public opinion. Neither are they a Christian witness.

In practice they tend to fall into two categories. There are those which set forth such vague generalities that they contain nothing distinctively Christian, are devoid of specific points, and in fact merely repeat what the government and the world expect of Christians! Then, on the other hand, there are those which are energetically partisan. These express an immediate and concrete judgment, but they are merely emotional reactions, naively partisan and inadequately thought out. In such statements there is an oscillation between theological principle on the one hand, and on the other hand, reactions which could be called journalistic. For a great many of the participants in congresses, synods and committee meetings there is the feeling of not having accomplished anything unless a "statement" has been issued.

How often have we heard the criticism: "People in the Church are spending their time on such things as the liturgy, the ministry, etc., when there are urgent questions, like Algeria, torture . . ."? Such talk is purely and simply an echo of the world's judgment which, however obvious it may seem to be, is nevertheless false. It is related to the celebrated ironic judgment leveled at the Byzantines, who were debating theological problems (in particular that of the Trinity; not necessarily that of the sex of the angels!) while the Turks were surrounding Constantinople. But we have only to ask: "What, in the final analysis, is the really important

thing for the whole of mankind—that Jesus is indeed
the Christ?—or that the Turks defeated the Byzantines
in the early fifteenth century?" These latter saw the scale
of values quite clearly. It was far more *urgent* to know
who was the Christ than it was to protect a temporal
city against an ephemeral invader.

So today, it is far more important that the Church re-
cover her sense of identity as the body of Christ, and
that she draw the necessary conclusions from that fact,
than that she should issue statements without weight or
significance, statements which are in no sense a presence
of the Kingdom, but which, more often than not, are a
way of easing the collective conscience about events for
which one feels responsible without being able to do
anything about them.

This need for statements is connected with another
sign of making the Church political, namely, *the passion for the latest thing*, about which we have already
said a few words. This passion which, in Christians as in
others, comes from an addiction to the press, television
and radio, produces, alas, the same effects in them as in
everyone else—political illusion. Among these effects
are the inability to grasp a political or economic situation as a whole, a weakness of political thought, an ignorance of the various levels on which political action
takes place, and a blindness to the fact that the most recent and spectacular is always the least important and
the least decisive.

Now statements are never issued except as occasioned
by recent events, which means that their value declines
as rapidly as the events in question are forgotten (unless they are incorporated into a propaganda campaign
worked up by a given political group). It would seem

that at every moment the Church should know exactly what to say about every exciting occurrence. That is a false conception both of politics and of the presence of the Kingdom. The passion for the latest thing shows itself in the meandering wordiness of articles in our newspapers and magazines. Also, the proof *a contrario* is always easy to state: You do not mobilize Christians on behalf of the more important and fundamental but less spectacular questions which the big weekly publications never mention.

Another sign, and a serious one, of making the Church political, is the passion which Christians put into their speeches, articles and political attitudes. We can take note of the fact here, then come back to it later. It would appear that politically motivated Christians are much more impassioned, excited and tense in these political questions than other Frenchmen. They inject into it something tragic, serious and profound, which other Frenchmen do not (except for small, minority groups). A Frenchman, unless he be a communist or a fascist, always jokes a bit when he talks politics. He is not about to kill himself, nor anyone else, over a thing like that. He has a lively sense, both of the interesting side and of the theoretical side of every political problem. He likes to expatiate on it without believing in it. Alas, our Christians, for their part, act as in a matter of conscience. They are incapable of irony, and they always feel guilty of frivolity in the face of decisions on which the fate of millions of people (and the course of history) depends! They deliver their political speeches with an indignation, an uncompromising quality and a seriousness which are overwhelming. There must be total involvement!

For if they engage in politics, as we shall see later on, it is not out of mere interest, but out of a terrifying arsenal of motivations which compel them to experience a tragic agony in connection with every political event. This causes them to adopt a strained attitude in their relations with others and to come up with sharply defined judgments—in any case, with an impassioned approach. It is easier, for example, to discuss communism with an intellectual belonging to the Communist Party than with a progressive Protestant, and to exchange views on a political issue with non-Christians of divergent shades of opinion than with Christians.

Among the more fervent of the latter one soon becomes aware of the idea that politics constitutes a sort of ultimate issue. For some, not to engage in politics is a betrayal of the entire Christian life. Politics becomes a test of the sincerity of one's faith. The political order takes on such importance that all teaching seems to converge on this entrance into politics. Biblical passages which clearly have nothing to do with the question are interpreted in a straight political sense. One rejects (or forgets) those biblical passages which minimize politics, or which treat it as a sphere of activity which is evil.

The political issue becomes ultimate to such an extent that persons and churches are judged in terms of political criteria. An eminent Christian can say: "It is inadmissible that Christians adopt this position on the war in Algeria. There are limits within which options are open to Christians, but outside those limits no expression of the Christian faith is possible;" and a sort of excommunication has been implied. Similarly, numerous proclamations make it clear that Christians who do not become involved in politics are hypocrites.

Certain printed statements reveal (unconsciously, it must be said) that for a significant proportion of Protestants the only valid incarnation of the faith is the political incarnation. Individual virtue possesses neither meaning nor value. The only thing that counts is belonging to a class, which is an expression of a political stance. Let us recall that dreadful statement of a pastor who "understands" (and in fact adopts) the hostile reaction of workers toward a completely charitable and truly humble Christian woman who was, however, the bourgeois wife of an employer. What did her personal virtues matter? She belonged to the hated class! One would think oneself back in the barbaric days of group liability. Yet this is expressly condemned by Ezekiel, among others!

Other pronouncements show that the moment one speaks of "presence to the world" Christians translate this as political presence. It would seem that there is absolutely no other way to be present to the world than to engage in politics, or to belong to a union; or rather, every other way of being present to the world is considered uninteresting and unimportant. The world is reduced to politics.

This idea that, in the last analysis, politics is the ultimate in importance is never stated outright, because one knows very well that it is theologically false and one avoids coming out openly with theological error. But good theology is no protection against false attitudes and implied beliefs, for this implied option is found in letters of theological students (1962), in the ostracism practiced against theological students who fail to take a stand in politics, in similar attitudes toward members of youth movements from Algeria, in the fact that only political groups are functioning well (in contrast to Bible groups), and in the outright declaration that if the Church is to be split and ruined by the political issue, well, so what?

It is at this point that the magnitude of the political passion reaches its full significance. The argument often put forward goes as follows: "Christians support a variety of political trends. That is a fact. To keep quiet about this divergence is hypocrisy. Unity maintained by silence is false, deceitful and hypocritical. These opposed views need to be brought into the open, and we must risk the unity of the Church to do it. That is honesty." Let us stress the fact that such a policy involves a twofold risk of splitting the Church. There is not only the risk we naturally think of, that of a split between the political right and the political left. There is, in addition, the far more serious risk of a split between those Christians who fail to see, or who reject, the importance of politics (who believe that politics is secondary, or who have no political opinion) and those who are politically activated (whether on the side of the right or of the left).

But should we not ask ourselves whether the risk of splitting the Church, which is substantial and serious, is commensurate with the value and importance of political commitments? In other words: "Is it worth ruining the Church for politics?"

In the face of the variety of political options available to Christians there are, in fact, two attitudes to take: either we treat these options as relative, take the heat out of our political stands, defuse the issues (for they are really false issues!), and have each person accept the pros and cons—in which case there is neither hypocrisy nor risk of a split; or else we can indeed assign a higher value to politics, make it the touchstone of Christian sincerity, maximize the conflicts and implicate the confession of faith in specific and one-sided political inferences—in which case there is, in fact, the risk of a split.

I say that the guiding spirit of this latter approach is not honesty but sectarianism. The ease with which some take their stand in favor of a break can only be the expression of a sectarian spirit, in both senses in which it is possible to understand that word: the sense of cutting and dividing, and the sense of following (for, alas, they are following impulses derived from the world). I would not hesitate to stake the unity of the Church on a question of truth, but the political debate, the choice among political options, the presence to the world by way of politics is not a question of truth. This can be demonstrated as well from the standpoint of political reality as from the standpoint of the data of revelation. Political questions can be burning questions in the world, but if they are burning questions that is the spirit of the world. The One-who-divides, the Deceiver, he it is who makes them that way. To accept them as such into the Church is to obey that spirit.

There are those who remind us that in the sixteenth century there were Christians who "took to themselves the beautiful name of *Politiques*" (as one of them puts it), and they invite us to do the same! They are forgetting a minor detail: in the sixteenth century the *Politiques* were those who accepted the task of reconciling Christian enemies in conflict over religious issues, and in order to accomplish this they turned to a "higher" value, namely, the State and the Fatherland.

Now it was certainly dubious, from the theological point of view, to use the State as the reason for the reuniting of separated Christians. But today the situation is reversed. Now it is a question of risking internal division in the Church on political grounds. What the *Politiques* of the sixteenth century and our "political sectarians" have in common is, in point of fact, the attribution of supreme value to the State and to politics.

A final trait which brings out clearly the sectarian spirit is the high value placed on *one* aspect of revelation, of scripture or of theology. The procedure is always the same. One discovers (in terms of a sound theology and of a great respect for scripture) one point, one issue which the Church has forgotten, in which she is no longer active, about which she is uncertain. Such discovery is assuredly good and right, but the Church is slow to hear and slower to change. One puts the pressure on, focuses all thought on that issue and calls upon the Church to make a choice. Now, when the issue is central to the entire revelation (the incarnation, salvation by grace, the lordship of Jesus Christ, for example) the uncompromising approach is legitimate. But the sectarian spirit is seen in the way in which one single item (the baptism of adults, the gift of tongues, nonviolence) is put in the forefront, assigned an exclusive importance, placed (mistakenly) in the center of theological thinking and made the criterion of truth, in such a way as to blur the essential elements and to cause the widespread agreement on the bulk of the other questions to be overlooked.

These various signs of making the Church political are serious, and, alas, many others could be cited.

CAUSES OF THE POLITICAL TRANSFORMATION

There are a great number of causes for this movement and we cannot analyze them all. We shall leave to
one side the objective causes, that is, those stemming
from society as a whole as it reacts upon the Church.
Our social world is increasingly political. That the
Church feels this pressure, that she finds herself involved, willy-nilly, in this political society, is a fact
which has to be taken into account. That the Church,
in addition, is invited to become a political power is
also plain to be seen. She is invited to participate in the
crusade against communism, or to assist the government
in its own politics. She is invited to help bring success to
government loans (in France as in the Soviet Union),
or to support the government peace propaganda, etc.
Here again, the facts have to be taken into account, but
the Church's thought and decision in these matters are
considerably easier (at least in theory!). Therefore we
shall confine ourselves to internal causes. Why have
Christians become political? Why do they want to be active in politics? There is an entire hierarchy of causes,
from the best to the worst.

Obviously we must call attention first of all to the sincere and deep desire to be more loyal to revelation and
to obey God's will. The renewed awareness of the importance of politics corresponded to the rediscovery that
Jesus Christ is Lord. This lordship had to be shown
forth in concrete terms which would make it clear that
it bears upon all *"exousiai,"* all thrones and dominions.
It had to be said once again to the Power: "You would

have no power . . . unless it had been given you from above" (John 19:11).

This general outlook led to a more serious dependence upon biblical texts having to do with politics and with the meaning of the State, not only in the economics of the preservation of society, but in the economics of salvation. Even knowing all the studies of the subject which had been put out over the previous twenty years, it was impossible to be content with theological study alone. One had to get into the practical application, and it was not easy to find the exact approach which would express for our day what the New Testament texts meant for the Roman era. A number of attempts were made in different directions, yet always with the same concern and point of departure, which was beyond criticism.

As an extension of this, we come upon another cause relating to what we had mentioned earlier: the good and legitimate discovery that the convictions, sentiments and attitudes of Sunday cannot be separated from those of weekdays, that there is not one domain of the sacred and another of the profane, that worship should lead to practice, that declarations of faith should be incarnate in daily life. Now in this daily life we are the agents, or the governed, of the State. As such we encounter political issues in which we have to assume our share of responsibility. "It is impossible to preserve our piety, and our individual and parochial serenity, by abandoning the destinies of mankind and of the nation to the passions of our age. The sphere of the State and of public affairs is one of the sectors of the necessary mission of the Church." One could find hundreds of other texts reminding us of the continuing Christian vocation in the realm of politics. Here again, no reservations are possible. It is obvious, as I wrote in 1944, that the political realm cannot be thought of as off limits to Christians. These latter have to bring to that realm the witness of the faith in Jesus Christ.

But to this theological idea, to this concept of the Christian life, there is added the lively sense of responsibility of which we have spoken above. It is emphasized that the judgment of God begins with the Church. Therefore, the universal responsibility of the Church and of Christians toward the world is vigorously affirmed. This responsibility is not only that of preaching the Gospel, but also that of having a hand in the forward progress of society, in its preservation, in the expression of the Gospel in terms of justice, liberty and equality. There too, there is no separation between the preaching of the Gospel as such and the actualizing of it in political structures. Accountable on that score, Christians also feel their responsibility strongly, sometimes tragically, for all injustices, all tortures, all hatreds, all lies. Having gone that far, they then are led to ask: "In keeping quiet, do we not run the risk of failing in our responsibility before God and before men?"

So here we are confronted with a primary set of reasons which, in principle, I find beyond dispute. I know, however, that other Christians, for whom politics is the domain of the demon, treat it, without more ado, as something which it would be unthinkable and impossible to approach. I shall not discuss that position here. I think it biblically unfounded. But the great problem is how to translate the recognition of accurate theological formulas into actual practice.

Before broaching this problem we must call attention
to other motives which have turned Christians toward
political action. This second category of causes is more
practical and immediate. It explains, for the most part,
the *direction* taken by the attempt to put into practice
the principles enunciated above, the outlook and the
viewpoint of political action.

First of all, we find a concern which is very close to
that of evangelizing. It is to the effect that one must go
out to meet people. They must be found where they
are, and we need to share their interests. Thus is emphasized, quite rightly, that there is where the mission
is, that we must not wait for people to come to church,
or to meetings organized by Christians. To evangelize
means to go into groups and meetings of people who are
not Christians. To evangelize is to declare a Gospel
which enters the concrete interests, the anxieties and
hopes of these people. It is not a good news which is abstract and spiritual.

But this is immediately interpreted as meaning that
people are assembled in political parties and in unions,
hence that is where we must go. People's interests are,
above all, political, and we must share those political interests with them.

If the point of departure appears beyond dispute, the
ensuing judgment of fact seems to us to be grossly in
error. In the first place, it is not true that "the people"
are in parties and unions. Not 10% of French people of
voting age are enrolled in a party, and only a very small
minority of workers are to be found at union meetings.
Can we say that *there* is where we meet "the people"?
The ones we meet there are the militants, the hard core,
the committed, the functionaries of the parties and un-

ions, those who are wedded to a specific ideal, to a hope, to preconceived judgments and stereotypes, that is to say, those with whom dialogue is just about impossible.

They also are those who have their own tactics, and who will only accept contact with Christians on the basis of those tactics. They scarcely need a hope (they have one already), nor an answer (they think they have it). Will one really meet "the people" at a tremendous mass demonstration made up of tens of thousands of "partisans for a day"? Since the encounter takes place during the course of that *kind* of activity, it can in no way be an occasion for serious witness.

Therefore this outlook leads, on the one hand, to a neglect of "the people" who are not enrolled in any party and who are truly without hope, are truly lost in the dead end of everyday life, and on the other hand, it leads to a political commitment which is one-way only, because the enrolled and militant French are all leftists. (The parties of the right are parties for rallying and electioneering only; hence they exist only at election time.)

This first error leads to a second. One starts out to witness to the Gospel, but one encounters people who are set in their ways and unmovable, the "rich" in the New Testament sense of not being in need of anything, of any good news. They have it! In this situation the aim of evangelizing gradually fades out, to be replaced by the idea of "presence." In the last analysis, this is but one presence among many others. One tries to let it be known that Christians are present *on behalf of* others, that they are not indifferent to other people's problems, that they are quite open to their arguments and are

ready to submit to questioning, and that as far as possible (but we shall soon see that this has its limits) they
are attempting a dialogue. One then pretends to scorn
what is known as "fishing," and one engulfs the quite
simple question of conversion in a moving and grandi-
ose panorama of world history,* set forth with an
impressive display of virtuosity.

One passes judgment on a certain number of the
themes of traditional preaching (redemption, for example) for the sake of eliminating them, explaining that
they mean nothing to people today, and that in order to
engage in the famed dialogue one must stand on the
other person's "natural ground," must accept his definition of things, of history and of the world, must become
involved on his ideological level. It is indeed true that
one must stand on the level of practical living of the
person, and must share his joys and sorrows, but to accept his interpretation of the world and his ideological
concepts is quite another matter, and that is one of the
standard procedures of heresy.

Against all this, we must insist rigorously that the
preaching of the Gospel has as its sole meaning the hope
that a person should come to know the grace available
to him in Jesus Christ, that through this he should
come to recognize that Jesus is truly the Christ, the Saviour, the Lord, in other words, that this person might
be converted to the true God. The presence vis-à-vis the
world of Christians and of the Church, the presence in

---

* It is quite significant that, in an important report on evangelization,
everything should have been made to turn on the concept of Jesus
Christ as Lord, and that the question of the Saviour should have been
passed over.

the midst of men, has no meaning, no value, no truth, unless it brings a person to this conversion.

It is of little consequence to have a part in the reign of justice *according to the world,* or to preserve the world for itself, to set up an economic or a political organization in which a person would be a little more happy, a little more free, etc. All that has no significance in itself (and I know full well that everyone will agree immediately on this point). It likewise makes no sense with respect to the coming Kingdom of God. It only has significance in relation to the following questions: "Will the human obstacles to preaching be thereby lessened? Will our witnessing to Jesus Christ with a view to converting people be more genuine and sincere?" Apart from this concern for conversion, all political activity is vain. With regard to the scorn for "fishing," let us simply remind ourselves of the joy in heaven over *one* sinner who repents, and let us not be more demanding than the Lord.

But there is another cause for political involvement, namely, what we might call "the Barmen complex." At the famous Synod of Barmen, in 1934, the Church saw clearly, and said what had to be said on the political situation in Hitler's Germany. However, we must remember that up to that point the Church had not taken a prophetic stance, since, in effect, the vast majority of German Protestants were for Hitler from 1931 to 1933 (we shall refer later on to this widespread lack of political clarity on the part of Christians). It should also be emphasized that the reaction of the Church at Barmen was provoked by the direct attack launched by Hitler against Christianity and against the Church. Granted these two qualifications, it is still true that what was said at the Synod on the subject of political power, and what was said to the State, was superb.

But, since 1945, French Protestant intellectuals have been dreaming only of Barmen. The Reformed Church in France must manage to say something just as good. That, undoubtedly, is one of the unconscious reasons behind the urge to issue statements. One dreams of the day when he might finally say something as decisive in the Reformed Church of France. It is generally forgotten that we have never been in as decisive a situation as that of Germany in 1933. This also explains the exaggerated and grandiloquent style used in statements about every event in French politics. In all good faith, parachutists are transformed into SS troops, de Gaulle into Hitler, the CRS (the police units created in 1945 to maintain order) into the Gestapo, etc., etc. The Barmen complex naturally leads the French Protestant intellectual to take his stand with the left (a second boost in that direction), since Barmen was a great stand in opposition to fascism (hence in opposition to the right).

Finally, we must take into account a second set of motives. One yields to the sociological tendency whereby the Frenchman, even when he scarcely takes any part in politics, still is convinced that all is settled at that level, and that everything depends upon the State. He loves to talk politics, without its meaning anything in terms of real results. Christians share this belief that everything is political and should be carried out and decided by the State. There is a kind of cloud of confusion surrounding politics, a political obsession according to

which nothing has significance or importance apart
from political intervention and, when all is said and
done, all issues are political.

We are faced, then, with a strange confusion of history and politics. History is "made" at the level of political action. All of us are called to take part in the
making of history. Therefore the only real action has to
be at the political level. We shall have occasion to dispute this notion, but let us simply observe here that it is
a direct participation in the beliefs of the century in
which we live.

In addition to that, the general current of our society
is toward the left. Leaving out of account electoral fluctuations, which are secondary, it is clear to any student
of politics that France has become steadily more socialistic over the past thirty years. We need only observe,
for example, that the "revolutionary" program of the
SFIO (the non-communist international socialist organization) of 1921 is completely fulfilled today, that the
"revolutionary" program of the CGT (General Confederation of Labor) of 1934 has likewise been put into
effect. All the socialistic demands of yesterday are realities today. It is obvious that the unions occupy a place
of growing importance among public institutions, and
that the problems of the working class have become the
most consciously important problems of our collective
psychology. The overall trend, the sociological inclination of our society is to the left.

Every reactionary government is obliged to declare
for the left, and what is more, to adopt measures advo-
cated by the left! Thus we have the third factor which
causes Christians to take a leftist position politically.
They are content to go with the tide (I do not mean to

imply that those rare Christians on the right are any more virtuous. They merely give evidence of a lack of realism and of a failure to comprehend the political facts).

Finally, the Christians who tend to make the Church political are the intellectuals, and here again they are following the general current. As intellectuals they all bear the stamp of Sartrian existentialism *, and that existentialism involves one in politics. One adopts, then, the theme of involvement, which is on everyone's lips and in all the thinking of the young intellectuals from 1945 to 1950, no matter what their individual leanings. One reacts like any other intellectual, and since one is a Christian one seeks (and finds!) a complete set of Christian connotations in this watchword.

Such appear to me to be the multiple causes, valid and invalid, all intertwined with one another, which are bringing about this political transformation of the Church with which we are faced.

THE BIBLICAL QUESTION MARK

The current analysis of biblical passages relating to the State, to the political power and to the attitude of the citizen, seems to me to present two weak arguments. We are reminded of the importance of the State in the economy of salvation. Barth's doctrine of the *"exousiai"*

---

* They are seduced at the outset by the common spirit of resistance and by the breadth of thought. They were also exceptionally vulnerable to the existentialist label. Recognizing that the biblical view of man and of the world is existential, and rediscovering the Kierkegaardian existentialism, how could they help looking with favor upon Sartrian existentialism, which contains so much truth, in addition to the seduction of success and of being in style?

is well known, and we shall not go back over that. But in the passages relating to the *attitude* of Christians we find only exhortations to obedience, to respect for the authorities, to prayer for the powers, to recognition of the honor due the king, and especially the exhortation to do good, since the ruler is there to protect the good. That is all there is.

Obviously, the attempt has been made to extract a political meaning from passages which have no such bearing, and to show that the words "moderation," "zeal," "order," "good behavior," etc., have a political significance. But that really is an exegesis so odd, and so in contradiction to all the other biblical teaching, that it should be resolutely avoided.

Now from this very minimal teaching on the subject of politics there are those who would derive guidelines of behavior which are quite far-fetched. From passages on the validity of the power one first draws, by extension, conclusions in favor of the validity of the modern State, and then in favor of the validity of political action generally. From passages relating to respect and to prayer one draws broad conclusions in favor of active and positive participation, in favor of action in the political domain. We consider this to be entirely unjustified.

In the first place, the biblical teaching definitely indicates two things: that the political authority has been willed by God as part of the plan of salvation, but that, at the institutional level, this applies to *persons* only (the ruler, the king). Let no one say: "It is that way because that was an age in which the power was personalized." The system of the *Polis* was still in existence, and the *Respublica* had not disappeared. It is an historical error to claim that if the Gospel writers spoke only of a personal power that was because there were no other kinds. The Romans had a fully elaborated abstract doctrine of the State. Hence we need to ask ourselves why these passages mention only the persons exercising the power, and never the *regimes*.

As a matter of fact, there were at that time great discussions on the royal government and the protectorate in Judea, or on the government of the *Respublica* transformed into a principate, and in process of becoming the Empire. The biblical texts are still further away from making any mention of a preference among *institutions,* a fact which would seem to indicate that it is quite exaggerated and unjustified to apply these texts, without more ado, to the modern State; and merely because the latter is the recognized holder of political power to treat it as equivalent to the king or the ruler spoken of in the texts. There is a difference of nature here, and if one is the least bit serious he can make use of these passages only with extreme caution, and with the greatest difficulty.

But the situation is even worse when the attempt is made to stretch this teaching to make it cover the validity of politics generally. The current tendency, in fact, is to forget those passages which used to be emphasized in the opposite direction: the condemnation of the establishment of political power in Israel (1 Samuel; Zechariah 11:6, etc.), the vanity and futility of political power in Ecclesiastes, the statement that the control of political power is in the hands of Satan (Matthew 4:9), Jesus' declaration that the leaders of the people are oppressors (Matthew 23:4). Finally, there is the general teaching that all political powers are destined for annihilation and judgment, in Paul (1 Corinthians 15:24), where it is quite clear that *every* rule, *every* authority and *every* power will be destroyed by Christ (without any distinction between the good and the evil *exousiai*), as obviously in the Book of Revelation (where it is very certain that the political power and all political institutions are swallowed up in the judgment of the great Babylon).

Therefore it does not go without saying that participation in the world of politics is a good thing, and that the Christian ought to be involved in it. To be sure, we must not jump unconditionally to the opposite conclusion either. If we are to understand the biblical teaching respecting the political power we must bear in mind the twofold teaching, the twofold judgment and the twofold meaning of what has been revealed to us. We must not exclude one of the two.

For example, it is precisely the demonic character of the power which makes prayer the most important political action that the Christian could possibly take, prayer which is a sharing in the struggle of Jesus Christ, prayer that the authorities might be brought into subjection, prayer that they might be exorcised, prayer that their power might be turned toward justice and good. Prayer is much more important than all the declarations, demonstrations, elections, etc. That is only one example.

If the Christian is to do more than respect and obey, he must in any case realize that he is entering the most dangerous territory, a demonic domain; for if the authorities have been conquered by Jesus Christ, they nevertheless retain, throughout the duration of our history, their demonic capabilities, their power to rebel against the Lord, their tendency toward evil through disobedience to the order assigned them by God.

We do find in scripture the establishment of dialogue between the prophet and the king, but active participation is rare, and is almost always associated with awkward compromises (Joseph, Daniel). In all scripture, political *action* is either absent, or is made to appear secondary. If we leave to one side the politics of the State of Israel, which is important only because the Chosen People are both State and Church, we see supreme indifference on the part of Jesus, and the greatest discretion in the epistles.

One hesitates to bring up the obvious fact, which nevertheless is generally forgotten, that Jesus paid no attention to problems of politics. He definitely refuses to take the lead in the Jewish nationalist movement. He recognizes the authority of the invader. He advises the normal payment of taxes (which was then a burning issue with the Jews). He displays an indifference toward the question of taxes, showing its unimportance by the story of the fish (Matthew 17:24ff.). He welcomes "collaborators" and traitors, and at no time does he take a stand against the numerous political scandals which were rampant in Judea. Jesus says nothing against Roman torture, or against crucifixions (of which we know, from several examples of that era, that the sentences were sometimes unauthorized!), or against extortion.

The only political statement to be reckoned with is in the exchange with Pilate, and we should note two things about that: the declaration that, when all is said and done, the power exists only because God gives it; and Jesus' indifference with regard to the power itself, which he does not contest ("My kingship is not of this world"). When we recall the extreme political agitation in all Jewish circles at that time, the popular excitement, the political parties which divided public opinion, the rebellions, the nationalist feeling, the evocation of the glorious history of the Jews in the demand for independence, etc., we are forced to acknowledge that, for Jesus, none of these things made any sense nor had any value, nor was the Roman authority any better or more legitimate in his eyes. It was simply there, and because it was there, one had to grant it a certain validity and see behind it a decision of God. "There is no authority except from God" (Romans 13:1). But that does not imply that one is to attribute a supereminent value to that authority. It can change tomorrow, and perhaps be just as good. But it was not the business of Jesus, or of the Christians, to change the authority.

If now we consider the passages in the epistles, we are struck by the small number and the brevity of these texts in comparison with the bulk of the theological and ethical teaching. That does not mean, to be sure, that these texts have no importance! But they are part of the ethics, a small part, and it is not legitimate to make them central, or to place them in the forefront, or to give them monumental importance, like those on baptism or on speaking with tongues. In any case, these texts provide absolutely no basis for involving Christians in active participation in politics (to be sure, they do not forbid it either!). They contain no directive for the Christian life about voting, or belonging to a party, or winning public office, etc. All the teaching, rather, is in the nature of restraint, of wisdom, and of a spiritual attitude, with all due respect to those who think there is *no* separation between prayer and action, for example.

I am familiar with the pseudo-historical argument advanced to explain this restraint, and the claim that it is no longer applicable in our day. It is alleged that at that time there was no such thing as a political life, that the inhabitants of the Empire were "subjects" and had no occasion to participate actively in politics. That being the case, the epistles could not allude to something which did not exist. But, so the argument goes, that situation has changed radically, and we cannot draw inferences from those texts, because now we are citizens called to take our part in a political life which does exist.

Now this widely held idea is mistaken. It is historically untrue that in the first century after Jesus Christ there was no active political life in the Empire, in which all were called to participate. The latest research shows, on the contrary, what had long been known, but only vaguely: that an intense political life did exist in the cities of the Empire (and not just in Egypt). In every city there was a popular assembly with very broad powers, electoral, financial and even legislative. Those popular assemblies were very much alive. It is known, for example, that at Ephesus, or at Corinth, there was a very elaborate democratic organization with political parties. Likewise, at the provincial level there were regularly, at that time, general citizens' meetings held under the presidency of the governor to study the administrative problems of the province. Finally, in Greece and the orient the old popular assemblies, the *koina,* had not been abolished, and in the municipalities the inhabitants were asked to elect their representatives, who were to meet once a year in the chief town of the province.

Do we see in the epistles of Paul or of Peter the slightest allusion to these various assemblies, elections and deliberations? Is there the slightest indication that Christians were to participate in them? Do we see any political orientation of a positive nature? One might, too hastily, argue that the worship of the emperor and sacrifices to the gods took place in those assemblies and that Christians did not attend them for that reason. The debate over that problem in the Church is a known fact, but *at a later period*. Paul would certainly have mentioned it if the question had arisen. But the question did not arise, because there was not yet at that time a true emperor worship, but only a ceremony in honor of the *genius principis*.

What are we to say of Rome? After being eclipsed at the end of the reign of Tiberius, the *comitia* were revived, and the emperors made efforts to restore some of their original importance. Does Paul, in the Epistle to the Romans, encourage Christians to take part in the Roman popular assemblies, to vote, to elect public officials, to decide in favor of this or that law? There is not one word of that sort, in spite of the presence of the political indications with which we are familiar. So all we can say is that, here again, there is a great indifference with regard to politics, and there is no encouragement to take part in them (which would have been entirely possible). Politics definitely does not appear as the favored arena in which to incarnate the faith, as some try to demonstrate today.

On the contrary, it seems to me that when one consid-

ers these texts in their historical setting they signify that
in politics, as in all the rest of life, Christians have *another* life to live: "Whereas everyone votes, proposes
laws, looks for ways to overthrow governors, attempts
revolts, draws up petitions, watches over finances, etc.,
you Christians have something different to do. You are
to be scrupulously loyal, you are to accept the decisions
of the power (even unjust ones), you are to pray, you
are to reject only the demonizing of the authorities, etc.
That is indeed a basic task *which no one is bothering to
perform,* and which will not be shown forth by attend-
ance at assemblies, nor by votes and petitions." The
teaching of the epistles seems to me to define clearly the
limits of politics, to imply an offishness with regard to
political activity in favor of another attitude, one which
is much deeper, much more positive, much more decisive, but which obviously is not what is known today as
"involvement!"

HISTORIC METAMORPHOSES

Ever since the Church became a vast institution and
a sociological body, the problem has been raised of her
participation in politics. The Church has come face to
face with politics, whether in the overall relation of
Church and State; or in the attempt to find solutions to
particular political problems (for example, the legiti-
macy of the power, or again, the definition of a just
war); or in the active participation of the Christian in
political life in general. It is even quite strange to come
upon the currently widespread notion that the Church
has not interested herself in politics, and that Christians
have to be coaxed into it, whereas it is plain to be seen

that the entire history of the Church is made up of this bond and of this relationship with politics in general. But throughout her history, the Church has not always displayed the same wisdom that we find in the gospels and in the epistles!

Obviously we cannot deal with this development in its totality. That would require going through the entire history of the Church. We shall be content simply with some examples which illustrate *all* the possible stands which the Church, or Christians, might take in the field of politics, and which show that, no matter what stand the Church takes, every time she has become *involved* in politics the result has always been her own betrayal and an abandonment of the truth of the Gospel.

First example. Beginning with the third century, it seemed in the Church that the need clearly was to convert the upper echelons, the administrative leaders, the family of the emperor if possible, and to bring the political power around to the practice, not really of Christian politics, but of justice, truth, charity, etc. It was a question of the personal conversion of the people involved, the prefects and the emperor, to the end that they might carry out their political functions as Christians. There would not seem to be any conflict between the Christian life and the functions of a political leader. Hence, on the personal level, the idea was that the emperors and their counselors and administrators should be Christians.

This attitude based on personal conversion (illustrated later on by the relations between Theodosius the Great and Ambrose of Milan) accounts for the lack of understanding in the current discussions carried on by

historians on the subject of the veracity of the Christian
politics of Constantine. What is certain is that, even at
this level, where it is simply a matter of the personal
conversion of the political leader, the Church finds herself under the necessity of bringing political judgments
to bear, which in turn leads to the Constantinian process. No matter how independent the Church might wish
to remain, she finds herself, from that moment on, inevitably tied to the decisions of the power, since the latter
(sometimes quite honestly) is seeking to put into effect
a Christian truth.

Under those conditions, how can the Church deny to
the power her advice and support? We are much too
quick to conclude that those politicians were Machia-
vellians from the very start. There were quite honest
ones among them who really sought to make their political actions expressions of their faith. But their very attempt meant implicating the Church in their decisions,
and it would have been a disgraceful cowardice on the
Church's part to have declined, to have turned her back
and to have washed her hands of the matter.

Now this brings about very rapidly an institutionaliz-
ing of the situation (Constantinism, the normalized
Church-State relationship), and also a casuistry, in the
degree in which it is impossible for the personal behavior of the political leader to coincide exactly with his
conduct as a public official, and in the degree in which
the Church recognizes her technical incompetence in
political matters. (A distinction will be made, for
example, between her competence *pro peccato* and her
incompetence *pro principe*.) From that point on, there
emerges the idea that the Church is a power which
should either guide the political power because she is

the guardian of truth (the Augustinian political theory), or she should collaborate with the power, with a view to the triumph of Christian truth in both the spiritual and the material spheres (the theory of Charlemagne, in which the pope was the inward bishop and the emperor the outward bishop), or she should be obedient to the power in the political order (the theory of Marsilius of Padua: since the power is of God, it should run the political society; the Church, as a part of that society, should function in the interest of the plan established by the State). There can be no other than these three hypotheses, at least to the extent to which the power openly declares itself Christian. This causes the Church to concentrate on the political problem, and from that are derived all the errors of Christendom.

Now we must not forget that the motives which led Christians along that path from the third century onward were exactly the same as those we encounter today among Christians who are politically aroused, and who suppose that political stands are decisive implications of the faith. We suffer from a tendency to settle too readily the account of the Church from the fourth to the thirteenth century by charging off her "errors." It can be said that the theologians of that period examined all the political problems, all the theological possibilities, all the possible Christian attitudes toward politics. To be sure, there is neither uniformity of doctrine nor conformity on the part of the Church.

In the Reformed Church today we are far from having thought out the problems as well as they, and their lesson is one of radical failure. Their failure teaches us that there is no such thing as a Christian State, that Christendom is not an answer, but also that the Church

can make no valid judgment in politics, that she can
only open an area of questioning. Apart from the most
rare and exceptional instances, she cannot take sides.

The same errors which were committed during that
period with the best intentions, the desire to be faithful,
the anxiety to bring the Gospel to bear on the actuali-
ties of life, all these we see reproduced within the
framework of French Protestantism. The moment the
reform moves into the political realm, one can say that
the betrayal of truth and of charity is already taking
place.

One such moment was at the time of the formation of
the Huguenot Party. Faced with the Catholic threat,
the indecision of the royal power, the numbers of Protestants, the persecutions, one came to locate the problem on the political level. For one thing, there was a
bodily defense which had to be established. For another
thing, there were political issues to be resolved, and a
certain need to influence the authorities. Here again, it
is oversimplifying to say that the nobles used the reform
movement in their struggle against the king. The fact is
that the action arose also from the pastors and the faithful. The third-century idea surfaced again: "After all, if
only the king were converted!"

But we know that precisely when the Church carried
the dispute to the political arena she also began to be-
tray the truth. She also sought to become one of the
powers of the world. She employed the same methods as
her adversaries: on the one hand teaching loyalty to the
king, while on the other hand stirring up all kinds of
trouble by her actions. She abandoned the focal point of
preaching in favor of social moralism and economic success. The problem was the same as in the third century.

The moment the situation lasts for any length of time, or one becomes a social body, one is driven to organize, to make a place for oneself in the world, to establish a political *modus vivendi*. At the same time the world itself has to be set straight, and what is too blatantly anti-Christian has to be eliminated so that a viable relationship with the State may be established, in which the State should pay attention to what the Church has to say!

From that starting point we encounter three trends. One is that of open conflict with the State when the latter turns persecutor, and the terrible epic of the Camisards is common knowledge. If ever there is a time when the Church seems justified openly in saying "No" to the State, and in employing every means at her command, it is when the State seeks to *suppress* the Church and the truth of revelation. We know how, at the time of the Camisards, religious prophecy gave birth to political prophecy. We know how political action, which is a thousand times justified on the human plane, leads to heresy (the overemphasis on the reign of the Holy Spirit, which is *always* a temptation for the Church when she enters this field), how it leads to a scandalously anti-Christian behavior and to a loss of the sense of charity. It is not for the Church to make use of political methods in her own defense. That has already been said countless times in the Old Testament!

It would seem, then, that only two ways remain: either work to change the State, or else collaborate with it and support it. We know that the first of these ways was adopted by the reformed French in the eighteenth century. They became increasingly sensitive to political issues and to the possibilities for changing the State.

That coincided with a growing reduction in serious theology. One was concerned to put forth a Christianity
which would be "acceptable" to the rest of mankind,
and so one leaned toward natural religion, discarding
absurd dogmas in the process.

Granted that the explicit viewpoint was totally different, nevertheless we see the same concern at that time
that we are examining today, the concern to encounter
man, the rational man of the eighteenth century; the
concern to speak to him in his own language (that of
natural religion, or today the language of myth); the
concern to influence the political world of the State by
taking sides as a Christian and by making "true Christianity" consist of decisions which are in line with progress, with "the enlightenment" (which corresponds exactly with the Church's conformity to socialism today).

To be sure, in order to do this it will be necessary to
give up a whole set of elements in Christianity which
appear to be superfluous. It is interesting to note that in
the eighteenth century, just as today, there was great opposition to the doctrines of the fall and of the radical
corruption of man. But that is a normal consequence of
the attempt to act on the political level, and on ground
common to all. Nor was this concern absent from the
Catholic church of the Middle Ages, with her rehabili-
tation of the light of nature and her doctrine of the
reason.

Finally, the eighteenth-century Protestants adopted
an attitude which is noteworthy because it is characteristic of our situation. We might call it "conformity to
tomorrow." It consists in a moderate opposition to the
existing political power, together with the espousal of
the ideas and doctrines of the most sensitive, the most

visionary, the most appealing trend in the society. This
is a trend which, from the sociological point of view, is
already dominant, and is the one which should normally be expected to win out (like the trend of the phi-
losophes in the eighteenth century and the socialist
trend today). In this way, the political stand has the appearance of being independent, whereas in reality it is
the expression of an avant-garde conformism.

We know the absolutely catastrophic consequences,
for the Church and for revealed truth, of the political
position of Protestants in the eighteenth century. All
the denials, all the divisions, all the compromises made
their appearance in that period and during the revolution. It is really a miracle, an unheard-of grace of God,
that the Reformed church should still have been sus-
tained by God after all that! It is useless to say that
there is an essential difference between the eighteenth
century and our own day, namely, the present concern
for the Bible and a sound theology. That is no lasting
guarantee, as I have already said, especially in view of
the fact that in our Church there is serious risk of losing
both, precisely because of the passion for politics and
the determination to be involved. In any event, the concern for politics displayed from 1750 to 1795 ended by
bringing the Protestant church into collaboration with
the State, of which the Napoleonic system is the proto-
type.

Now it is indeed noteworthy that we find, on the part
of the Church authorities, the same arguments, the
same motives, the same interests, the same "theological"
reasons for supporting the Napoleonic State that we
encounter today in Church bulletins from Hungary and
Czechoslovakia for supporting the communist State

(one even finds praise for the emperor's will to peace). It is too easy to say that Christians in those days were weak and lacked seriousness and clarity of vision, etc. We were not there. They only shared the prevailing atmosphere of their social environment and of their times (and that is all they can be faulted for), just as we share ours. Collaboration led inevitably, as all history testifies, to subservience to the State. The latter, necessarily, will use the Church to further its own ends (the preaching of morality and obedience to the laws, as Napoleon said).

That is the way it is in the Soviet Union, in Hungary, in Czechoslovakia, together with, may we say, some additional hypocrisies, namely, the justifying use of "good" theology (for some of the theologians of those countries are quite profound, which was not the case with the pastors of the Napoleonic era), toleration of the anti-Christian propaganda of the State, against which no one is taking a clear position except in East Germany, and acceptance of the prohibition against evangelizing. The fact is that those churches agree to being limited to individual piety and spirituality (especially the Russian Orthodox church) and they never escape from it since they contend, meanwhile, that it is essential to be involved in politics, to support the decisions of the State, to justify them theologically and to be of service to the State's propaganda.

In the final analysis, every time the Church has gotten into the political game, no matter what the manner of her entry, no matter what her opinion or opposing choices in a political situation with regard to an institution, she has been drawn every time into a betrayal, either of revealed truth or of the incarnate love. She has

become involved every time in apostasy. When all is
said and done, it seems as though politics is the
Church's worst problem. It is her constant temptation,
the occasion of her greatest disasters, the trap continually set for her by the Prince of this world.

The proposal is made to the Church on every occasion to give expression to her faith in the political
order, to act effectively, for once, on the course of this
world through the avenue of politics. She is forever
being reminded that she cannot remain a stranger to
the actual life of people. And she walks, each time, precisely into the blind alley of abandoning what is
specifically hers, her unique vocation. Each time she is
transformed into a power in bondage to the world.

*Yet we must continually remind ourselves that the
opposite attitude has not more truth on its side.* The re-
view of successive historical betrayals by the Church
through political involvement does not signify that the
Church ought to be spiritual, that the faith is a matter
of the personal and the inward, that revelation is purely
abstract, that the contest for truth has no political implications and that the love imperative has no social significance. All that spirituality is just as false, treasonous
and hypocritical as the taking of political sides condemned above. It is a negation of the incarnation, a forgetting of the lordship of Jesus Christ. It is to scorn
one's neighbor (whose life is affected by the political,
the economic and the social). It implies that we acqui-
esce in giving a free hand to the Prince of this world. It
is the rejection of everything Jesus tells us about the
Kingdom of Heaven. It is the *other trap* which Satan
lays in the path of the Church.

If I do not elaborate on that criticism it is because it

is one that is being made just about everywhere (and I have made it myself in a number of writings over the past twenty-five years). It is also because that temptation does not seem to me to be the principal threat to the Church *today* (which certainly was not the case for the Reformed Church of France around 1930).

5

How Choices Are Made

Everything considered, the first question which needs to be raised is: "Is there a Christian political doctrine?" The great majority of Christians engaged in politics will answer: No. There is no one political doctrine which expresses Christian truth exhaustively, and for that reason there cannot be a political party capable of bearing the name Christian. That leads to the conclusion that Christians will choose from among the world's political options, and so will enroll in non-Christian political parties or groups. In this way they will be faithful to the obligation which we have discerned of carrying the presence of the Gospel everywhere.

But in that case we have to ask ourselves what the motives are for which Christians make a given choice of direction, and what kind of behavior this involves them in. In the end, the motives which are advanced with

more or less clarity boil down to four which are distin-
guishable from one another even though frequently intertwined.

THE STATED MOTIVES

It will be said by some that we must become involved
in a political party, or a union, for the sake of being
there as Christians among men, and in order to witness
to Jesus Christ. The implication is (though this is seldom stated openly) that one is engaged in the work of
conversion and that the connection with the Gospel is
therefore a fundamental one.

Others will see human sympathy and relations with
people as the reasons for involvement. One must be
part of the social or political trend, without too much
reference to Christianity but still for the sake of the witness of love.

Still others will give ideological reasons for becoming
involved, on the ground that there is a certain affinity
between a given political, economic or social doctrine
and the thinking, theology or ethics of Christians, so
that one opts for a certain viewpoint out of theological
conviction.

Some, finally, and this last motive must be carefully
distinguished from the preceding one, believe that in
the world as it now is the faith carries with it implications in favor of a certain social action. Hence one will
join with those who support that attitude and share that
viewpoint.

We need to examine the consequences of each of
these points of view. After that, we must look into the
real motives, hidden behind the ideological pretexts,

which cause Christians to go in a particular direction. In the process, we shall leave to one side the first of the four, the only one which seems to us to possess Christian validity. That motive we shall study in detail in the final chapter, as a positive approach recommended for adoption.

So let us turn now to the second motive. It adds up to saying that we are Christians, but we are living in a world which is what it is. It happens to be one in which we have little chance of introducing the faith, yet we must be involved in it (from the standpoint of the faith itself). We are living in this century, so we must make our decisions in this century. We must choose on the basis of those motives which appear humanly to be the most valid. I am in a world given over to violence. One violence answers another. I have to choose that violence which seems to me the most acceptable. I am in a world of special interests. I have to choose that interest which seems to me the most just. To be sure, I am a Christian, and that necessarily will weigh heavily in my choice, but it is still as a human being that I choose one of the world's parties.

This attitude, encountered *very* frequently, is nothing other than the well-known and much denounced distinction between weekdays and Sunday, for underlying this distinction there is always that "painful necessity" of living in the world and of choosing one's side, on the theory that, after all, it is the least evil side. It is worth noting that this very old and very bourgeois attitude is in fact adopted by those Christians who are the most involved and progressive. They are the ones who claim to be crusading precisely against that same distinction, but who fail to consider the implications of their attitude. The same procedure which formerly left the door open to the world of money now leaves the door open to the world of politics. In spite of all the excuses which are put forward, we must (just as has been done with regard to the bourgeois and his business) look squarely at the facts.

For example, do Christians who are active in their party demand absolute truth? Certainly not! We know any number of statements signed by Christians which contain manifest lies. Do Christians command their opponents' respect? We know the many notices posted by Christians which foment outright hatred. Do Christians introduce into their party or union relationships differing points of view for conscientious discussion? It seems that this does happen, but it can hardly be said to be very frequent or of very weighty significance. Otherwise those Christians would simply be thrown out, something we seldom hear of. Thus they are free to make any mental reservations they want to. They bear the label, and that is it.

Here we have the very criticism so often leveled at those Christians who participate in the capitalist and bourgeois society: "Oh of course, individually you can carry on your own little personal activity which no one knows about, but you leave the total outlook of the system completely unchanged, and you yourself take part in it." That is exactly what can be charged against the Christian who is active in one of the parties. The fact is that whenever one claims to be establishing a "dialogue," or presenting a "challenge," the Christian always begins by accepting (out of a mistaken charity) all the other person's principles.

That was flagrantly the case in the colloquy between

communist and noncommunist intellectuals. The non-communist Christian intellectuals were so chosen (before the dialogue could even take place!) that only slight shades of opinion separated the two groups. The noncommunist intellectuals had already subscribed in essence to the communist doctrine (the dialectic of history, the meaning of history, a condemnation of capitalism, the necessary advent of socialism, etc.). After that, they were free to introduce all the shades of opinion they wanted! For the listener who was both noncommunist and non-Christian (as some of them have told me) that meant that in the last analysis *the* intellectuals (in general) and *the* Christians (in general) agreed with the communists on everything except "religion."

In the foregoing instances we have been thinking of Christians who did not believe overmuch in the content of the ideologies of the group in which they were active. Let us turn now to a second type of attitude (although we need to keep in mind that the diverse motivations are very often combined in one and the same person). There are those who choose, or who claim to choose, on the basis of the fact that in their eyes a particular doctrine corresponds to Christian thinking. One will favor the West and capitalism because it contains a safeguard of the individual person, of freedom, of a recognition of the Church as such, etc., all of which things are quite obviously Christian. Or one will favor the communist left because of its sensitivity to social justice (the expression of love), because it is the poor man's cause, etc., which things are no less obviously Christian. Henceforth one must, as a Christian, commit oneself to a particular political course because it expresses a

(Christian) truth at the same time that it constitutes a defense of a human cause. It is in the name of Christian truth that one will lend his support to that cause. So the Church, or the Christian, will take pains to show that that political course is in fact "Christian," or at least *more* Christian than others!

This approach, while it was formerly quite usual, is put forth less frequently today. One is being very careful. Yet the principle is reintroduced whenever a person explains that this or that viewpoint is the one for a Christian to adopt! Thus there is no political position which is Christian because "derived from the principles of Holy Scripture," but the Christian should choose from among the ten or so parties, or viewpoints, or doctrines, that one of them which in the last analysis best expresses the demands of revelation for all people today, in the current social context.

This raises a general problem which we can only mention in passing since it has to do with the whole of morality. If there is no such thing as a Christian ethic, then the Christian has to choose from among the world's values those which in his own day, etc. This is *in fact* (again, in spite of the denials and qualifications) the problem of natural morality.

Let us note that, at the political level, this is what the Church has always pretended to do, and as a consequence she has supported the most diverse systems, always justifying them on Christian grounds, and occasionally even by an entire theology. In the sixteenth century no one had the slightest doubt that the monarchy was the only theologically acceptable and justifiable regime. In 1793 a great many Christians discovered, with the aid of religious arguments, that in the final analysis democracy was the form of government to be desired.* But in 1804 Christians who were politically involved discovered that the imperial system was the most authentically Christian form, etc. Each time, there were very serious theological arguments to show that one was supporting a given system for the sake of Christian truth.

This is far from disappearing today. Once more we come upon arguments, either in justification of western civilization, or in justification of socialism. That leads us to point out, in addition, that Christians are not unanimous in their opinion, but are split into two main currents, within each of which can be seen subdivisions. Alas, that is not the result of a great freedom of choice, but of the fact that our society is itself divided, and that the strongest current, the current of the future, is socialism, while the other is still quite vigorous.

We must emphasize a new difficulty in this type of commitment. There are Christians representing divergent political tendencies, which they have chosen for their deep affinities with Christianity, and then they very soon identify these with Christianity. We have met with the same process under another aspect. Whenever in the nineteenth century, and in 1914, and even in 1939, the churches made common cause with the nation, the churches on each side assimilated Christian truth to national victory: "Gott mit uns." It goes without saying that each church did not think of itself as socially conditioned, but had rather the conviction of

---

* And we all know how often, since 1870, there have been, in France, arguments on the part of Protestants to prove that the Protestant system of Church government was democratic, and that Protestants had always shown a preference for that type of regime.

having made a free, existential decision of faith. Each church prayed for its country, and celebrated the *Te Deum* of victory. For the reformed French of 1939 it stood to reason that the struggle against Hitler was a Christian duty, but it cannot be forgotten that in that Hitlerian Germany one of the heads of the confessing church asked, in 1939, to be reinstated into the army. In spite of all the qualifications which he could have against the regime, the situation was the same as that described above: the Christian felt conscience-bound, and could not help identifying his cause with that of his country.

Of course we can say that today we are no longer celebrating the *Te Deum* of victory (but we should ask ourselves whether that is not simply a sign of the weakness of our national unity, and of the loss of certain ideologies). Yet we are seeing the same identification between Christian truth and political option. On the one hand there is extolled the anticommunist crusade in defense of Christendom, and on the other hand there is the claim that socialism is the hope of mankind, which the Christian should support. In many group meetings the prayer for justice sounds exactly like a prayer for socialism, and the understanding of the commandment of love directly implies the triumph of socialism.

There is a final motivation on the part of those who feel obligated to be Christian within a political course defined by others, but in which, on the whole, this or that aim or viewpoint (as defined by the world) *is* in itself an implication of the faith. In reality, that position has two sides.

For one thing, there is the theological affirmation of

the collective dimension of the Christian faith and its implication for politics. For example, one will say that it is impossible to be content with individual, personal virtues in living the faith. Thus a Christian cannot adopt a position with regard to money in his personal life (that of giving his money to the poor). Today it is necessary to translate that into an economic outlook, so that the Christian position on money should lead to the adoption of an economic concept of some kind (for example, an economy of equality, in which profit would be eliminated and work would be fully remunerated, in which there would be no economic oppression, etc.). Similarly, when one embraces the commandment of peace, that cannot remain personal and individual. It involves an obvious collective outreach in terms of participation in all pacifist movements. The examples could be multiplied.

But, on the other side of the coin, we also find the tendency (which we have already examined in chapter 3) to see "a decisive implication of the faith" in this or that secular movement: for example, the struggle against the atomic threat, aid to colonials in their revolt against those who colonialize them, the secularization of the schools or the growth of the unions. In those instances it cannot be said that they are direct and obvious extensions, by social application, of an immediate consequence of the faith. It is rather a matter of discerning, among the political viewpoints, that which is in agreement with the faith.

Now we maintain that, all things considered, this is *a return to the concept of application of Christendom,* that is, to an overall, universal concept of society, of economic life, of political life, which is supposed to be just and right in accordance with Christian truth, and which leads to a rejection of certain other positions as inadmissible. Such was always the attitude of the Roman church. Moreover, one comes upon a perfectly logical hint in this direction by a Protestant author: "The Catholic church well understood those things when she indirectly inspired the creation of the MRP [a Roman Catholic-oriented socialist party], of the CFTC [a French confederation of Christian workers], and other less well-known bodies, thus providing herself with instrumentalities . . . with which to apply her ethical instruction to the body politic. But we (Protestants) are still too timid and hesitant." Ah yes! Whenever you come to the point of stating clearly the consequences of the faith in economics and politics at the collective level, whenever you become involved in a choice among the world's political viewpoints, which is supposed to be theologically based and strict, you are indeed obliged to develop political instrumentalities for putting them into effect.

It is impossible to rest content merely because society is turning in that direction, that is, when society is in process of constituting itself on the model suggested by the faith. It would, in fact, be an absurd contradiction to say that the faith calls for a given economic structure, or a given political decision, but that, as a matter of fact, Christians do not seek to put it into effect!

Now, what we are told is precisely that these decisions are also perceived by others, that one does not have to be a Christian to discover and promote them. By and large, it is said, one can locate the just solution to a political or economic problem through reason and good will. It is that solution which the Christian sees as an implication of the faith, so that everyone can be involved in the same quest and action for the guidance of society.

But such a view of things is exactly that of the Middle Ages.* It is a vision of a society in which the political decisions, the social and economic structures, would be the fruit of the involvement of faith, to which all men can aspire, to which they can belong and in which they can all have a part on the strength of their natural reason. That is precisely Christendom. There too, as our Protestant authors present it to us, one considers social duty equally as important as individual duty. Moreover, our authors go much further than that when, for example, one of them writes the remarkable concept that "active membership in a union is just as important as conjugal fidelity." Surely the theologians of the Middle Ages had a better theology of the married couple and of love based on Ephesians. But for them, too, involvement (at that time corporate), and a just price, were essentials.

We are reminded of them again when we meet up with the idea of a "just war," so prevalent among our Protestant intellectuals in connection with the war in Algeria. By the application of different criteria, some are able to show that it is a just war, others that it is an unjust war. But the concern to establish criteria for a

* A number of authors who feel that one should take a stand on some economic or political problem think to avoid Christendom by saying that it is a matter of taking a stand *hic et nunc* on a specific question. Now this simply does not follow. One cannot come to a serious decision on an economic problem except in terms of an overall economic concept or doctrine. Now, if we state or support that position as Christians, we are supposing that it ought to be applied to the world as an expression of the faith, and that is necessarily a return to Christendom.

just war already contains within itself all the potentialities for Christendom. We must not forget that, historically, it was in consequence of this problem that *everything* thereafter evolved.

Moreover, this implicit temptation to Christendom finds support in the desire to show that Jesus Christ is Lord. That, too, the medieval Church wanted to make known. How better could she have done it than by affirming the supremacy of the Lord's command over that of the State? After all, wouldn't we be quite happy to have the State follow the advice of the Church, and thus acknowledge that the Lord's commandment is the right one? Would we not have been very pleased to have had the State listen, at the outset, to the statements of the Church on torture, on the police, on the concentration camps in Algeria? Again, the desire to witness to the lordship of Jesus Christ in politics would imply, for example, that Christians should assume the leadership of a party or of a State, and should make plain what that means; or again, that they should propose an action so *different* from that of the ordinary political powers that Jesus Christ would be shown forth in that action as Lord. But in every one of these courses one sees, in the end, the emergence of an indispensable Christendom!

I am aware that those authors will be offended, because they are just as fiercely contemptuous of medieval Christendom (Alas!, it would appear to have been out of clearly evil political motives), but as a matter of fact that is exactly where they themselves are headed: toward a Christendom based on *their* modern view of things, a socialistic and technological Christendom.

Yet they deny that. On what grounds? Simply the fact that, since Christians are in the minority, and Protes-

tants only a tiny minority, *therefore* there is no danger
of Christendom. One is free to adopt all the theological,
political and economic positions which would inevitably have brought about a Christendom if Protestants
had the benefit of a preponderant majority. One can
adopt them without any qualms. Their implied Christendom can be put aside as of no consequence, in view
of the fact that there is no chance of such things coming
to pass with the Protestants in the minority. So one can
preach forceful sermons urging Protestants to become
active in politics, for the outcome will never be more
than an individual affair, satisfying the needs of the
conscience. There is no risk of its being put into effective operation, or if it were so put into effect it would
be the others, the non-Christian politicians or unionists
who would implement it. That gains our end at minimal cost, because the giving of our support to their
struggle makes it the (implicit) expression of the lordship of Jesus Christ.

THE REAL MOTIVES

Again, we need to be clear about the real motives
which can cause a Christian to decide in favor of a
given solution for society. We are very quick to say that
it is an implication of the faith. When I read innumerable articles written by Christians, of the right or of the
left, on the war in Algeria, I nowhere find them expressing the faith. What I do find are political choices
made for entirely human reasons, in which the Christian differs not the slightest from the non-Christian.
When it was stated that the incorporation of Algeria
into France was inadmissible, that an independent Al-

geria was the only just solution, that the rebel chiefs should be accepted as accredited spokesmen, etc., I find in these statements numerous political presuppositions and a sociological outlook, but not a shadow of a particularly Christian insight. The same is true of the statements insisting on the imperishable rights of France to remain in Algeria, the nonrepresentative character of the FLN made up entirely of rebels, and peace through an accord of integration. There are as many "Christian reasons" on one side as on the other. The options are worked out on the basis of factual judgments and political presuppositions, under sociological pressures.

The factual judgments of Christians are induced in accordance with their special sources of information. I know in advance that the reader of *l'Express* or of *l'Observateur,* who does not read the opposing newspapers, will take a certain position. He treats as information whatever is passed on to him, and that information conditions his judgment with mathematical precision. It is taken for granted that news items stemming from the government or from the *Figaro* are nothing but lies and propaganda; and conversely. Now the facts which are entertained as such (on the basis of a prior, irrational belief and confidence placed in a given source) can indeed produce this or that "Christian" reaction, which is then grafted onto the predetermined political stance. At the bottom of all these positions there are political presuppositions which depend, in turn, on temperament, on private passion, on environment, on a given education, none of which things originate from a "Christian" milieu but from the social group common to all.

The political decisions of Christians hardly ever

come from their theology or their Christian thought. If they did, there would at least be a body of minimum agreement, but no such consensus exists. That means either that Christians choose their political positions without reference to the content of the faith, or that a spiritual judgment has to be made between good Christians (known by their good political decisions) and false Christians. We have observed that the sect of the politically active is quite prepared to make that judgment.

What we really see is that Christians adopt all the possible political positions, and we have no right to suspect their good faith, nor their Christian faith, nor their ability to live that faith. That must mean, therefore, that the choices are made for reasons which have nothing to do with the faith. There are purely personal factors; for example, a character sensitivity to a given value. A person will center his position around freedom, or justice (which, in today's actual world, entails a variety of political attitudes), peace, self-esteem, etc. There are strong feelings resulting from personal occurrences. A Christian moved by a deep-rooted hatred for de Gaulle will rebuild his entire politics around this feeling of resentment.

But one's milieu and station in life are even more determinative. Christians make up their political minds in terms of their situation. Their judgments are defined by their sociological milieu. The *pied noir* is going to react in terms of his milieu, that of the French in Algeria, and in terms of his station in life as a *pied noir*. Normally he will favor a French Algeria, and in extreme cases will support the OAS [secret rightist army organization in Algerian war]. This is readily granted by Christian intellectuals living in France, to whom it is quite plain that there is very little that is Christian about that attitude.

What they fail to see is that they, too, are reacting in terms of the sociological trend and of their own station in life.* Christian students are going to react like the rest of the student group. They will adopt the same lines of argument, the same judgments, and will believe the same statements of fact. They do not think in terms of their faith, but in terms of their student situation, the more so since, in the case of the Algerian war, for example, student opinion follows the inclination of their conscience. They can put values and humanism in the forefront (freedom for oppressed peoples, justice, pacifism, etc.), which conforms to the general tendency of intellectuals.

Yet they do this in the degree to which *they are not* in the situation of those who are living through the affair in Algeria. That is to say, there is no conflict between their station in life and those values. Quite the contrary. The values go along with their self-interest, which is not to go off to war in Algeria. That is cruel. But at the same time one perceives a sensitivity to any change of milieu. A student who, in Paris, is very active against the war in Algeria, undergoes a complete reversal of opinion once he leaves for Algeria. Are we to say that this is due to his having been "propagandized"? The fact is, he had been "propagandized" before. He was ex-

* To say that "it is impossible to safeguard our piety . . . by abandoning the destinies . . . of the nation to the passions of our age" is true; but Christians might well ask themselves whether they are not obeying the passions of their age in attributing such importance to the nation!

pressing his Parisian student environment, and the opinion of his weekly newspaper. Afterward, he will give expression to his new environment, that of the army. It is exactly the same thing,* and we encounter these changes of opinion at all levels.

An intellectual Christian, very active on the left, full of energy and conviction for the independence of colonialized peoples, leaves for Black Africa. After a certain time he returns, his ideas completely reversed. He has come into contact with realities other than those he had "seen" from a distance when he was in France. To be sure, it should be emphasized that his attitudes are very seldom determined by direct, personal self-interest of an economic or pecuniary nature. Yet they are determined through his belonging to a milieu.

Honesty should lead us to acknowledge that the political stands which are taken are defined by the objective life situation. I see nothing wrong with reacting as a bourgeois when one is a bourgeois, as a working man when one is a working man, as a *pied noir,* as a student, as a man twenty years old or as a man seventy years old. What is intolerable is the pretense on the part of Christians that their conditioned attitudes are the result of the faith,† when they cover their political stands with a cloak of theology, when they make a display of Christian motivations, and when they say they are acting and

---

* When I say that it is an expression of the station in life and the environment, I do not mean that it may not be at a sacrifice. The members of the Jeanson group, like those of the OAS, paid with their persons, but that does not mean that they were giving expression to a personal truth!

† What was, above all, unacceptable in the position of the OAS was that "in all good faith, Christians cloaked themselves in Christianity in order to carry on their activities." (Msgr. Guéry)

deciding in politics as Christians, all the while that they are really acting and deciding as (very independent) politicians! The falsehood and hypocrisy begin when one declares that a French Algeria, or the independence of the Algerians, represents a Christian cause.*

Someone will retort: "But isn't that going back to the old dichotomy, Christian on the one side and politician on the other, with a watertight bulkhead in between?" I think not, for it is a question of seeking *another* way, *another* connection, *another* political significance. But that search can only be undertaken after we have recognized the original fixing of our choices and ideas by our environment and life situation, after we have given up covering our purely political and sociological positions with a Christian cloak and have accepted all the consequences which that entails. For example, as long as one says that the solution of an independent Algeria is the only one which gives promise of justice one can *rest assured* that no thought of the Christian faith in politics, no stance of a Christian person in politics, is going to be invented. The evil is not in the taking of a stand, but in the use of Christian reasons to justify it.

The depth of the tragedy is shown by the one-sidedness of the judgments of Christians. They plead values. They plead truth, justice and charity, but only on behalf of their political friends. They vigorously denounce torture and crimes which have been committed, but only those committed by their political enemies. Of course they will acknowledge that their friends commit some crimes or offenses, but they hasten to gloss these

---

* On this subject I refer the reader to the splendid letter from a pastor in Algeria, published in *Réforme*, February 24, 1962, which is the only sensible thing written on the subject.

over and to find an excuse. The rightist Christian will say: "Look at the atrocities committed by the FLN," (and he will cite thousands of cases of butchery and torture). "Obviously the OAS people are wrong . . . but you cannot expect everybody to put up with threats indefinitely without striking back . . . The number of their offenses over the past six months is infinitesimal compared with what the FLN have been doing for seven years . . . You must understand people driven to desperation in a tragic situation." The leftist Christian will say: "Look at the shameful torture and the fascist crimes, etc., etc. Obviously there have also been offenses on the part of the FLN, but, in the first place, that does not directly concern us because they are Muslims. Let's sweep our own doorstep first, and begin by faulting Frenchmen and Christians . . . There is a violence which liberates, etc., etc." One will acknowledge that one is fighting for freedom, but one will not accept the same motivation on the part of one's political adversary. My greatest sorrow is to observe the fact that, for political Christians, the political adversary counts for nothing, in spite of hasty and evasive claims to the contrary. One completely forgets the command to love one's enemy. Even there, hypocrisy slips in. How often have I heard Christians of the left say that they love (and help) the Muslims because they are "our" enemies. How can one help being scandalized by that, in view of the fact that the Muslim is the leftist's friend, being the enemy of a hated regime, of a condemned economic system and of an execrated colonialism? Love of neighbor has nothing to do with help extended to the FLN by Christians of the left. I still await on their part an attitude favorable to members of the OAS, since the

OAS is the enemy of the Christian leftist. That is where the love of one's enemies should be exhibited. I do not know whether any Christian leftists have rescued OAS leaders from the police, as they have done for the FLN. What they say on behalf of the FLN is that "one must help the fugitive asking for shelter, and save him from eventual torture." The same argument, exactly, goes for the OAS. Alas! the rightist Christians are the ones who will help them.

An intellectual will declare, in the same breath, that we must favor nonviolence (whenever the violence is against his political friends), but that violence should be employed against those who threaten democratic liberties. Another, who has taken a strong stand against torture, could still say to me, in connection with tortures inflicted on members of the OAS: "I don't see why anyone would want to protect those people who fired mortars into a defenseless crowd . . ." On the other hand, it is to the great credit of the magazine *Esprit* (May, 1962) that it forcefully raised the question of torture inflicted on fascists.

A synod will proclaim that it is impossible to justify systematic anticommunism on the basis of the Gospel. I agree; but the same is true of antifascism. Conversely, fascism cannot be justified by the Gospel any more than can communism. But that is not said! To be sure, it can be argued that if we strike a blow against the right and then a blow against the left in this manner the Church is not saying anything. That is true. But if the one-sided judgments arising from options which are purely and simply political are inadmissible, and if, on the other hand, the Church is "saying" practically nothing when she speaks to the right and to the left simultaneously,

that really means that the problem is being wrongly
stated, and that in accepting the options proposed to us
by the world, by society and by the environment we are
going nowhere.

The political problem needs to be thought out in a
different way, in different terms, along other dimen-
sions and on another level than that on which it is currently being thought out and presented. It is a question
of considering political reality, not from the standpoint
of a so-called concrete situation set forth by pseudo-
news items, which are always inadequate and serve to
mislead rather than clarify, but from the standpoint of
a certain number of scriptural commandments, from
the standpoint of the revelation concerning the world.
In most of the judgments and stands taken by Christians in these matters, it is the *point of departure* and
the *method* which are at fault.

If, upon analysis, there is no such thing as a Christian
political doctrine, if political stands are dictated by
human motives, and if they consist in choices from
among entirely human solutions, that fact should put us
on our guard with respect to two things.

The first is the ambiguity and confusion of the witness which Christians think to bear when they intervene in this domain (since, as we have seen, that is one
of the motives most frequently put forward). Are we to
suppose that when a pastor signs a manifesto, indicating
his title as pastor, or even when he speaks at a political
meeting, that he has borne witness to Jesus Christ
(even if the speech is quite clear and Jesus Christ is explicitly brought into it)? From oft-repeated experiences
we know the real significance of that sort of thing.

Doubtless the Christians who are present can rejoice at the thought that the Church is at last present in the people's midst. But the non-Christian? Will he hear a message being preached? I say (apart from a miracle) *never*—and that by the very fact of the situation. Those people have come *for the purpose of hearing* statements in favor of French Algeria, or against the OAS, and they listen to that for which they came. They hear what they came to hear. The motives of the speakers, or the call to values, or the raising of questions, those things are of no interest to them.

Psychologically they are incapable of hearing them. All they remember, all they *can* remember, is that the Christians agree, on the whole, with the ideas, the catchwords and the propositions contained in the order of business or presented in the meeting. To the man in the street, the political presence of Christians does not signify a call to conversion, or a recognition that all issues are subject to the lordship of Jesus Christ, but simply: "The Christians are on our side."

The whole thing rests on a dreadful confusion and ambiguity. If Christians are asked to be present among politicians, that is for the sake of their moral certification, which helps avoid certain criticisms. It is also for the sake of the effect on segments of the population attached to Christianity, because the Church in the end represents a degree of power as an institution. As has often been said, Christians in this situation are hostages. If it were merely a matter of our persons, it would not be important, and I would keep quiet about it. But, as a result of our intervention, it is God's truth which is being held hostage, which is being used as a pretext, as a justification, as a means of propaganda. That is why we are driven to the point of no compromise. We have to say "No."

Someone will object by saying that the Holy Spirit *also* can act in these circumstances, so that the witness may be listened to and received in spite of everything. Obviously . . . but if that argument puts an end to all discussion, it also puts an end to all endeavor. It is hard to see why one would bother evangelizing, for example, if one could in that way fall back on the incomprehensible action of the Holy Spirit! The Holy Spirit does not do away with the human argument, with the evaluation of situations and means, nor with personal involvement.

Finally, coming back to what we were saying above, political choice is purely human, and Christians ought to know that. If the choice of purely human solutions is being made for reasons of taste, or passion, or conviction, or sociological pressure, there is a final conclusion to be drawn which is of major importance. We must acknowledge the very relative and secondary nature of these questions. We must acknowledge that if the Christian faith forces us to become involved in political activity, as in every other human endeavor for the sake of being with people in their lives and in their tragedy, nevertheless revelation supplies no answer to politics. On the contrary, it treats it as relative.

Hence we, too, should treat all political endeavor as relative. We can never take part in a "final struggle." We can never accept nor demand ultimate sacrifices. For example, we never have the right to participate in meetings or movements which ask the execution or the massacre of the worst political enemies, because nothing decisive or final is ever involved, or gained, or risked in politics. We have to remember that, even though the

Eternal has entered into history, that is not in order to eternalize history. It is the *Eternal* who has entered into history. Politics thus becomes one activity among others, which does not put it so far above the conduct of one's private life.

Politics boils down to being a problem area in which we, *as Christians,* have our part to play. But the first decision incumbent upon us is precisely to let it be known that it is only a problem area. Therefore we reject all overestimation of political decisions, all idealizing of any political regime, and by the same token all execration (*ex-sacrare*) of another. We owe it to our political friends to protect them from the inflation of words. After all, whether Algeria remains French or goes politically Muslim is a relative shift. The final destiny of France does not hang on either solution. All points of view have their motives of justice and their burdens of injustice.

The only thing that counts in the end is the suffering of the people involved in these conflicts. That suffering is strikingly shared on all sides. I cannot resign myself to the humiliation, the subjugation and the economic misery of the Muslims under French domination, but neither can I resign myself to the massacres of Europeans, Jews and harkis, or to their being dispossessed of their goods and torn from what was for them a fatherland.

This cannot be weighed quantitatively. There is no such thing as a just war. It can never be the war of the Eternal which we are waging in our political conflicts. It is shortsighted, both politically and spiritually, to say that there is a violence which liberates and another which subjugates. All violence is a crime before the

Eternal. The end never justifies the means. Since only the Lord justifies, we need to remember that it is the same with political decisions as with people themselves: not one is *just,* but *all* can be *justified* in Christ.*

---

* I know very well that someone will say in answer to this that "all cats are not gray," and a political decision is not a matter of indifference, to be decided by the toss of a coin. That is obvious. But the differences are only relative, and they are only on the moral plane. The difference is the same as with people. Of course it is better not to be a murderer or a drunkard, yet we know that even when he is very good, man is still a sinner before God. "There is not one righteous. . ." So it is with politics. Now most Christians who are active in politics forget that. They turn it into an ultimate value. Even when they protest verbally that this is not so, their judgments and their behavior give them away. That is the real tragedy in making the Church political.

6

Incompetence and Irresponsibility

When one reads the articles which Christians write on political issues, or when one discusses such matters with them, one is generally, with rare exceptions, disturbed at their lack of competence and knowledge of the subject; and that includes the intellectuals. The latter are usually very competent in philosophy and are inclined to talk politics as philosophers, or rather to oscillate back and forth between philosophic reflection and the current event. This oscillation, this way of looking at things from two widely separate levels, largely explains the fact that Christian intellectuals take communism more seriously than anyone else.

In communism we observe the *same* duality. There is one viewpoint of philosophy and one of *praxis,* of current practice. In any discussion, communists are always referring back and forth from one level to the other.

We are familiar with the following type of dialogue: "Look at the increase in the standard of living in the Soviet Union."—"Perhaps, but how about the dictatorship and the concentration camps?"—"Yes, but the meaning of history and the elimination of contradictions?" Or this: "It is hard for us, as Christians, to accept materialism."—"Yes, but look at the economic democracy which has been achieved in the Soviet Union! Etc., etc." Now the trouble is that real politics does not take place on either of those levels, but on the ground between the two.

INCOMPETENCE

I hardly ever find Protestants speaking with competence on political economics, sociology, social psychology or political science. Certain leaders make an effort to read books of "documentation" in politics or economics, which is all very well, but what they fail to realize is that these are more often than not of a popular nature. When really important works are in question, these leaders generally pass them by (as their book reviews in Protestant magazines show!)—a result of their lack of fundamental training in those subjects.

It has not yet occurred to Christians that political thinking does not take place on the level of philosophic ideas. It presupposes, rather, a knowledge of a certain number of subjects, and a sufficiently rigorous method. In this day and age, it would never occur to Christians to send notoriously incompetent persons into a scientific milieu to enter into discussion with physicists and to take sides on some theory in physics, on the basis of a few general ideas and clippings from the weekly newspapers. But it is not yet realized that political economy, or politics generally, have become just as difficult (if not as precise) as physics, and that they presuppose knowledge and a method, which are not to be had from the reading of a few of the latest books, or a few weekly newspapers or magazines.

In the presence of this problem of competence, I am obviously aware of the argument: "Politics is everybody's business! To require competence in order to assess a political issue and take a stand on it is undemocratic." My answer is that I indeed want to see the most incompetent citizens decide, in the end, political issues. I am deeply democratic. I am not engaged in an analysis of the working conditions of democracy. That is not my purpose. I am only saying that *intellectuals* and *Christians* should refrain from speaking rashly on political issues.

Incompetence is inadmissible on the part of Christians who are committed as witnesses of Jesus Christ, when providing others with a sense of direction, speaking with authority and encouraging young people to become involved. It is not justified by the fact that "politics is everybody's business." Science also concerns us all, but that is no reason for our jumping into scientific debates! Christians must come to understand that it takes more than good common sense to comprehend a political issue, that philosophic ideas about the State are of no use at all (for example, to attempt to think through problems of politics on the basis of Hegel's ideas on the State, or on law, is as futile as it would be to try to understand nuclear physics on the basis of Lucretius).

But Christians allow themselves to be taken in by the

prevailing vogue. They see everybody expressing his own "ideas," so why shouldn't they do the same? That's all right as far as I am concerned, only let them be less pretentious about it, less authoritative, less inclined to expect everyone to follow in their wake. And let them not claim to be representing Jesus Christ! Am I being unfair and unduly critical?* Alas, all one has to do is to reread the books or articles written by Christians ten years earlier to see the vacuity, the inaccuracy of the political judgments, the superficiality, the ambivalence of the terms and analyses; and that is true even of books or articles which *seem* to be well informed!

In reviewing the attitude of Christians toward communists, we can take this very characteristic example: Where, in communism, is the really *political* thinking to be found? At the level of Lenin, and nowhere else (Stalin having faithfully perpetuated and implemented the thought of Lenin—as did also Khrushchev). But hardly ever do I find a Christian who really knows Lenin's political method, and who pitches his encounter with communists at that level. That is the only point of any consequence; but it is also the only one at which a rupture *can* take place. To discuss the pragmatics of revolution as applied to the current situation, or to draw inferences from political independence, and from the relativity of concrete decisions in terms of their place in an overall strategy . . . that is very embar-

* Little amusing examples: A certain Christian leader, who writes frequently on political issues, confuses the charter of the AFP with that of the RTF, even demanding that the RTF be reformed, which simply shows his complete ignorance of the facts. Another, who is very active in the unions, was entirely unaware that the Labor Exchange was anything more than the building in which the unions hold their meetings.

rassing. At the intellectual level it is uninteresting and very difficult. Those are good reasons for staying away from that sort of thing. The moment the political problem is considered at that level, the enthusiastic, philosophic discussions between Christians and Marxists lose all meaning.

This incompetence, evident in writings and proclamations, is even more apparent in encounters with the Christian who is actively involved in a party or union. His beginner's training is usually very deficient, both from the point of view of biblical theology and from the point of view of politics and economics. But once he is involved the situation becomes worse, for participation in politics is very fascinating and absorbing. It is not play. All one's time and energy are taken in committees, public gatherings, the drawing up of statements or propaganda leaflets, meetings, doorbell ringing, the posting of notices, etc. Opportunities for acquiring knowledge and for reflection grow less and less in proportion to the increase in conviction, confidence and unqualified judgments. Inconsistencies become progressively blurred, as well as the ability to think things through from the standpoint of revelation.

Then the Christian demands that church worship be made more liturgical, with more time for adoration and silence. The Christian life takes refuge in adoration and contemplation. Meanwhile one's political life is taken up with activities embraced within the party line or the union line. In other words, one tends unconsciously to play down the intellectual and thoughtful aspect of the Christian life (by reaction against the sermon and against biblical studies), since these might be in conflict with the activities one is pursuing. One then falls back on the conviction that it is sufficient to "be a Christian" implicitly or mystically. This "Christian being" gets into politics and becomes involved in its activities. That is supposed to constitute a presence (the salt, the leaven, etc.). In addition, there is the good conscience derived from the conviction that it is precisely in being present to the world, in being sent into the world, that one *is* a Christian, and faith grows in consequence. In this way one justifies all incompetencies.

The initial error has to do with the very word "politics." Not infrequently, in one and the same writing by a Protestant intellectual, the term will be used, without definition or warning, in three or four different senses, which leaves the door open to all kinds of slips and ambiguities (unintentional, I'm sure!). Sometimes it will refer to one's presence in all the activities of the "city," sometimes to relations with the State, sometimes to participation in political movements, sometimes to an involvement in history. Yet it would seem to me very essential that one distinguish carefully in a matter so critical and controversial. The ambivalence paves the way for the drawing of unwarranted conclusions from a biblical passage dealing with one aspect of the subject by applying it to another aspect, etc.

With certain authors, politics becomes "everything" when all is said and done. Adopting the Marxist idea that man is nothing more than a composite of social relations, one treats him as a political being only. Politics is then something which embraces all human activity. Moreover, that assumption is widely accepted in our society. From it one derives the notion that the only form of presence to the world is the political presence, so in order to carry out the responsibilities of a Christian in society and among men it is essential to "get into" politics.

That concept most certainly rests upon an anthropology which Christian thought is unable to accept, and also upon a confusion between "politics" in the sense of the affairs of the "city," all man's activities, and "politics" in the sense of an involvement in a political movement (a party or a politicized union). When Christians think in this manner they are only adopting the most dubious suggestions and beliefs which the world holds out to them in order to possess them. Far superior and more reliable is the analysis made by contemporary students of politics, when they research the "limits" of participation and conclude that politics has some character as a specialty. If there is not a restrictive threshold, a clearly defined line, there is at least a problem-area of political interest, which is limited, and a problem-area of interest in private life, which is also limited.

Another, equally distressing aspect of incompetence is the craze for what is current. Like everyone else in this society, Christians do their thinking, become worked up, and fluctuate in accordance with the latest news. For them, the political issue is unfortunately confused with the issue on which the news cameras are focused. Certain rudimentary factors are forgotten, namely, that news-reporting procedures are *all* warped and give *only* a distorted picture of reality; that it cannot be otherwise; that most current facts remain unknown to us; and that if one wants to understand a current item, he must dig deeper into a more profound reality.

But especially is it forgotten that there is a certain

carry-over, and that most genuine political issues are not those of the current news. Christians, of course, will make every effort to "keep informed." That was evident in connection with Algeria. They will read serious books on the subject. They will even study the economic or demographic background of the problem. But from the very start the mistake is made of supposing that the Algerian question is one which involves one's whole life, his responsibility, his virtue, his truthfulness, etc., etc., when, as a matter of fact, it is still a superficial, current-events issue, even when related to movements of anticolonialism and economic questions, etc. The Algerian affair was important for Christians when it was not a current-events affair, that is, prior to 1954. The concern over Algeria evidenced by *Esprit* in 1934, the writings of Camus, the Viollette Report, those had real significance. Unfortunately, Protestants were not interested, or so it seemed!

Now, to be engrossed in the latest news, to follow the popular lead in submitting to events and to the press is, for one thing, to resign oneself to not understanding anything (because passion clouds the judgment), and for another thing it is to resign oneself to total ineffectiveness (because once the event has burst into the open it is too late to do anything). To be sure, whenever I have had occasion to lay before Christian groups other political problems which are just as serious, deep-seated and real as those engrossing public opinion at the time, the standard reaction has been: "But we didn't know that!" Certainly one cannot know everything! The only fault I find here is with the belief that what one knows about is the most important thing, that what one knows about represents the whole of reality and calls for one's total commitment! In fact, what one knows about is very often only a *veil* which conceals the really important and decisive factors.

Also, in pursuing current events, Christians display that very distressing trait which modern man has of shifting his interest at the caprice of the daily news. We witness, in consequence, a sudden loss of interest right after an exasperating flare of enthusiasm. One fluctuates with the circumstances, convinced that politics is identical with "world news." The Church is urged to take a stand on a current matter, which she needs to look into from the political point of view (for there is no other criterion!) and which she is manifestly not qualified to assess; so she adopts a vague and uncertain position (it could hardly be otherwise), and the report which she issues on that current matter will forthwith be forgotten, not only because the Church has said something of no importance, but also because the event in question has itself been forgotten. Thus the work on Penelope's robe has to be begun all over again, even though it means nothing in the end. Every stand taken by the Church on a current political problem merely demonstrates the Church's weakness as an influence on the world. It also demonstrates the ignorance of Christians on the make-up of the political structure, and their ineffectiveness as a presence to the world.

Unfortunately, this causes Christian intellectuals to pose political issues in false and incomplete terms. Again, that is a product of the oscillation between general principles and current events. On the one hand, they accept certain political ideals (for example, the right of all peoples to self-determination) which they will base on philosophy, without any *political,* still less any historical, examination. These general principles then take on the nature of axioms. On the other hand, the involvement is at the level of the immediate event, without consideration of the broad context of the political situation and of its significance when looked at from a worldwide and comparative point of view. In this way the problem is stated in false terms, always to the neglect of the decisive factors originating on the median ground between philosophic ideas and the specific event.

At the very best, in the attempt to state a problem they will refer to a "specialist" on a certain country, for example. But the political phenomenon is one which cannot be entirely mastered by *one* specialist. Correspondence and collaboration among a number of specialists would be required, together with the application of rigorous methods supported by extensive knowledge. Otherwise the specialist on one country will yield to the inevitable limitations of a specialist. Obviously, such an undertaking, such an endeavor to examine the actual political problems at their true level, is neither thrilling nor exciting, nor does it hold the promise of the kind of involvement which gives us the illusion of doing something about them. Experience convinces me that Christians are not prepared to advance by that route.

FLUCTUATIONS

The superficiality of the political judgments of Christians stems also from the fact that they habitually allow themselves to be fenced in by the world's options. "There are only two solutions, either *this* or *that*." That is what the world is ceaselessly setting before Christians and telling them, and it always adds: "There is no other way." Now the Church should be there precisely to affirm that there is another way, that there is an option, unseen by man but infinitely real, that there is a dimension to the affair which is unknown to man, that there is a truth above and beyond the political alternatives which has its repercussions on them. Now when we look at the specific choices made by Christians, we see that they always revert to what the world has proposed. We wait for the world to take the initiative, then we approve or disapprove afterward.

Suddenly we find Protestant intellectuals placing their hope in a third power, or in neutralism, or in a Marshal Tito, or a Bevan, or in a Socialist Party. Now it is precisely when the Church lets herself be limited to the alternatives proposed by society that she becomes incapable of standing on the ground from which her own action would be possible. She can no longer speak as a Church, in the name of Jesus Christ. All she can do is to follow this or that crowd.

Another facet of this superficiality becomes evident when one sees the Church always falling back on morality in the political domain. (One is forever looking, among other things, for the famous Christian social ethics; and the Church wanders about as a sort of Diogenes.) It is always for moral reasons that she speaks and decides politically: "It is wicked to torture. Man should be able to eat all he wants. We must preserve our honor. We must keep our word, etc." That is all true, of course, but it is a useless thing to be talking about from the practical point of view.*

* "Study Plan on the Church and the Algerian Problem" (Reformed Church of France, 1960), was perhaps the only one which tried, without entirely succeeding, to think the question through in a different way.

To be sure, this taking a stand on the ground of the most current morality makes it possible to walk *shoulder-to-shoulder* with a great many people, and with all the humanists. Respect for the same morality allows one to share in a common action and to sign the same manifestos. But is the Church a society for the application of a universal morality? Is it so certain that the ethics derived from the faith correspond to the humanist morality? (I am not saying that the two are necessarily in conflict, but surely they are not identical.) In any case, to fall back in this way on morality is a striking indication of superficiality, and for two reasons.

First, it reveals an obvious lack of understanding and knowledge of *actual* politics (in contrast to that pictured by philosophers), and in particular an ignorance of the de facto autonomy of politics. One clings to the belief that politics is an affair of morals, and that the moral judgment *has a place* in politics, which is pure illusion. Christians can say, of course, that they reject that autonomy, but really to mean such a rejection they must first find out from experience how hard it is. It is easy to "reject" Newton's Law—but then . . . ? You don't accomplish it with words.

When someone rejects this autonomy he is merely putting together an *ought-to-be*. It is aggravating, in the first place, to have a Christian take a political stand as though this *ought-to-be* were an accomplished fact, or in such a way as to lead us to believe that it really exists, when it is only a figment of the imagination. In the next place, it would be important to know by virtue of what we are rejecting this autonomy in politics. We soon discover that the rejection is by virtue of moral "values." Yet it is precisely in that regard that the autonomy is most indelibly marked.

This brings us to the second reason for the charge of superficiality. The Church is called to bring a spiritual judgment to bear on the situation, to speak a prophetic word. Thus she is assigned a genuine role. In carrying out that role she cannot look for conscious collaboration from an external ally. She cannot "cast" her word into the mold of a common formula on a compromise platform. Her point of departure is not a moral judgment (not even that of the dignity of man), and she cannot give moral counsel. By reason of the fact that she operates on her own level, her word can challenge politics, not by entering it to play its game and win a bit of territory, but by showing up the inward contradictions and the harm of the autonomy of politics. She forces these into the open by radicalizing situations, which must always be the result of the action of the Word of God in the world.

Should we give examples of this superficiality of judgment on the part of Christians? Nothing shows it up better than the "fluctuations." Let us take some relatively old ones! A certain Protestant intellectual, today one of the staunch supporters of the Church's political involvement, said to me in April, 1938: "I don't understand your interest in politics. How can that possibly change the essential human situation? God's action is independent of the political contingencies. A change in the administration in no way alters the possibilities of God's action. To try to think through and become active in a political problem makes no sense for a Christian. Even in the presence of concentration camps, a Christian need not be so concerned, for he can remain free even in prison." Surely that intellectual has forgotten those statements of which I had taken note. Today he says just the opposite. Obviously the war has intervened, and that was the occasion of his about-face.

Shall we recall a certain book by a theologian, which was quite a sensation in 1947? Armed with full documentation and prooftexts in support of an accumulation of facts, the author explained that the communist regime was not at all what it was generally assumed to be. According to him, an extraordinary liberalization had taken place. It was false to be talking about a police state and concentration camps, etc., and, in effect, Christians should go along with the communists. A few years later this author disavowed his book, and acknowledged that he had been completely mistaken. But I wonder whether that is enough. The book had been a success. It had been read. Many young people believed it, and were involved in collaboration with the communists. The tardy disavowal had come too late. The harm had been done.

On a foundation of error, ignorance and emotional enthusiasm, a supposedly competent Christian authority had involved other Christians in a certain political activity. I say that that Christian authority bears a terrible responsibility. To be sure, mistakes are always possible. But politics seems to be the Christian intellectual's favorite arena for making (entirely avoidable) mistakes.

May I cite two impassioned articles from the time of the Korean War, vigorously denouncing the bacteriological warfare waged by the Americans, and showing to what horrible lengths capitalism was going? I recall being harshly criticized at a young people's conference for having said that this business of bacteriological warfare sounded to me like propaganda. Now Mr. Khrushchev has indeed stated that there never was any bacteriological warfare. Yes, but *the articles in question* did exist. They influenced the opinion of their readers. They had their part in the formation of political judgments.

Must I recall the attractive articles on Poland and Hungary, on the validity of the communist regime, on the cultural progress in those countries, articles which appeared in 1956 from the pens of various Protestant authors? All these articles were refuted by the Polish Uprising and the Hungarian Uprising. To my knowledge, only one of the authors has had the courage and integrity to say that he was mistaken, and had failed to see things clearly.

Let's stop there. I could multiply these examples, and could cite more recent ones! What is characteristic is that the change of opinion on the part of our authors always results from the intervention of an occurrence which refutes a previous judgment. Let us note, first of all, that in none of these cases was the problem so difficult or obscure that it would not have been possible to see with a little clarity. It was not superhuman. Here we are in the presence of Christians who have spoken loudly, firmly and clearly, at a time when they hardly had the competence to do so. They have been obliged to recant when the facts have revealed the inanity of what they had said.

What strikes me as especially serious is the fact that in such circumstances the changes of opinion were brought about as a result of events. Most of our Christian intellectuals give in to this, like any other intellectual who only finds out through an event that his earlier judgments were mistaken. It took the Twentieth Congress of the Soviet party to convince them that Stalin was a horrible dictator. It took the Hungarian Uprising to make them see that the Soviet Union is an imperialist power which fleeces its "people's democracies." It took Castro's explicit declaration to make them realize that he was in the Marxist camp and that he would be a bastion against the western system.

By that I do not mean that it is abnormal for a fact to make us think. Still less do I mean that we have no need to take facts into account! I do mean, for one thing, that extensive information is available, which makes it possible to gain a fairly accurate (if precarious and partial) idea of the situation, one which doesn't fluctuate with every change of event. Thinking which fluctuates in that way is characteristic of false information and of excessive dogmatism (a theoretical mind-set which prevents the appraisal of clues, of the less prominent data, and which refuses to give in until the catastrophe has burst into the open, when it is too late).

Those communists who changed their minds after the Hungarian Uprising merely demonstrated that they had previously been communists for the wrong reasons (from the Marxist standpoint), and that they were giving up communism for equally wrong reasons. They had neither a sufficient knowledge of the doctrine nor sufficiently rigorous habits of thought. It is the same with Christians. To be sure, something can always happen which takes everybody by surprise, like the success of the Bolshevik Revolution in 1917, but the examples I have chosen, and those which I could take from the past four or five years, are not in that category.

Now this strikes me as quite a serious matter for Christians. Their thinking *could* not fluctuate as it has if, for one thing, their approach to politics were guided by a true concept of the world and of politics, if it were *based* on that instead of on uncertain choices from among the world's options; and if, for another thing, Christians realized that their faith implies the careful observation of fact (if they applied to the socio-political scene the great theological imperative: listen before you talk!). Quite obviously, they probably would have a harder time making up their minds, and they would keep quiet more frequently. It is pertinent to wonder what harm that would do. After all, what does being present to the world mean, from the standpoint of the truth and responsibility of the Christian life? Does it mean "saying just about anything, so long as you say something and people listen," or does it mean very often: "Keep quiet and pray!"?

IRRESPONSIBILITY

We come now to the last stage of this (for me) painful examination of conscience (of myself, of my Church—from which I in no wise separate myself—and of my brothers, whom I consider to be no different from me!). Unfortunately, Christians very frequently act like irresponsible persons in the political domain. That attitude of irresponsibility is evident to me on three levels.

First of all, in consequence of what we have been saying, it seems serious to me that Christian intellectuals, pastors and leaders of movements, should adopt

very definite and clear-cut attitudes in politics, and in
whatever has to do with the presence to the world, when
they are so unsure both of the theological foundations
of their thinking and of the validity of their political
judgments and information—in short, when they are so
incompetent.

For them to decide on their own personal positions,
and to keep them as their own, is well and good. That is
only the normal · exercise of freedom of opinion. But
here they are thinking of themselves as leaders, writing,
publishing and presenting as certainties what can, at
best, be considered tentative hypotheses. In so doing,
they drag many of the faithful in their wake, especially
the young who place their confidence in them. I call
that an irresponsible attitude.

For when, two, three or four years later, events bring
these intellectuals to acknowledge that they had been
mistaken, the damage is done. Those who followed
them are committed to that course. If the leader then
says he was mistaken, they can no longer change the situation. Those who were shunted to that track three
years earlier will remain on it! Whenever, through the
theme song of a Christian intellectual, young people
have joined the ranks of the OAS, or a group supporting the FLN, which is exactly the same thing,*
whenever these young people are put in prison, or even
risk being killed, for the wrong reasons, badly thought

* I do not mean by that that the OAS and the FLN are intrinsically
the same (I would discuss that point elsewhere), but rather that the
involvement of the young people I know in the one or in the other is
of the same kind, is brought about by the same reactions, is induced by
the same type of irresponsible adults, and is entered into with the same
blind passion.

out by Christian intellectuals, I say those intellectuals
are responsible for what happened. Yet they have acted
as though they were not responsible (even if, at a trial,
they ask to be condemned *along with* the young people
they have involved). Their duty as Christian intellectuals requires that they take care to know what they are
doing, instead of yielding to impulse, to emotion and to
political persuasion.

This irresponsibility is also seen in the fact that
French Protestants constitute a tiny minority, and
hence are exceptionally free to adopt political positions
which are sometimes quite startling, sometimes uncompromising, and sometimes complex. They are free to do
this because, after all, there can be no mass effect.
There is a rather painful absence of realism in our declarations and in our political stands, which comes from
our inability to implement them. How could we implement them, since we are only a handful, and divided at
that? To be sure, that is not the idea in the minds of
those who stand up for their convictions, and who demand that the Church lend her support to this or that
position, but it is nevertheless in the background of all
Protestant political talk. We can, as a matter of fact, say
anything we please. There is no risk of our being taken
at our word.

Bishop Dibelius said to me somewhat bitterly a few
years ago: "You French Protestants can say anything because it doesn't involve your whole nation, whereas
whenever our synods, or even I, speak, there are millions of Germans who could alter the entire politics of
the country." Such is, in fact, the comfortable position
of a member of a sub-minority. He can adopt the most
extremist positions because he is only involving an ex-

tremely small group. That approach is healthy, *provided*—and here is where our examination of conscience comes in—provided one doesn't offer it as an example for all to follow, and doesn't say: "This is how *the* French should act." That setting of a pattern is hypocritical, because one knows in advance that it will never be followed, so one's conscience is at ease.

Now for the third aspect: irresponsibility with respect to the government. Christians occupy the comfortable position of a permanent opposition. They are forever lecturing the government on the basis of "good principles," but either in total ignorance or in an idealistic misconception of the actual political circumstances. Obviously, I am not alluding to the debate over Machiavellianism, which is still entirely theoretical and abstract. But, once again, the current political scene is not the one our intellectuals who take sides think they know. Political decision, at the centers of political decision, in the possibilities open to it and in its procedures, is not what they suppose (and here again, these intellectuals, philosophers and theologians arrive at their conclusions on unreal grounds, yet they give young people the impression that *this* is indeed the political reality!).

The advice they give the government and political administrators is generally quite impossible of realization. I do not deny the *moral* validity of such advice, but I reject the falsehood that such a position is workable in practice.

Taking it one step further, if it were workable, the advice they give to governments would be catastrophic in terms of the price to be paid. I have often heard it said: "If it costs a lot, so what?" (For example, to abstain from the use of torture.) "We need a humane and liberal approach, etc." * "If it costs a lot, so what?" is the prescription of a person who is not obliged to make the decisions. Over and over again we have heard these clear-cut statements in the line of the opposition. Then, when the opposition comes to power, it behaves otherwise. Power corrupts man? Yes, but to locate that corruption on the moral plane is too simple an explanation. It is ridiculous to explain it in terms of wicked capitalists who are about to seduce the leftist ministers. Quite simply, when one is in the position of making the decisions, the burden is slightly heavier than when one is giving advice. It's a little more complicated than one had previously supposed.

Many, and I too at age eighteen, confronted with the rise of Hitler, declared: "The only approach is that of complete pacifism. France should set the example of unilateral disarmament, no matter what the cost! If France is occupied by the Germans, so be it!" In 1940 we found it wasn't as easy as that! Moreover, it was the most ardent pacifists of 1936 who became the most ardent members of the resistance. Let's not say: "Yes, but in the case of Hitler's Germany it was obvious that . . ." No. It was no more obvious in 1930 than the dictatorships of Khrushchev or Tito or Castro today. The students who, in 1935, showed a 90% majority burning

* A very interesting study could be made in connection with impressive statements about the necessity for soiling our hands by becoming involved in the political realities. Those who make such statements are the first to recoil in horror when there is really dirty work to be done, and they are the first to condemn those who perform the base tasks. The truth is, what these philosophers mean by soiling their hands is the signing of "petitions which set forth high principles of morality, humanity, etc.," and lecturing others. Unfortunately, a different and more serious soiling is involved.

with enthusiasm for *l'Action Francaise* and fascism bore a blood resemblance to the students who, in 1960, burned with enthusiasm for the United Socialist Party and the Soviet Union. Their arguments were neither more nor less valid. They were expressions of the same search for the same values.

I say that when a person has no responsibility to exercise power, and has no direct and actual share in it, that person should be moderate in his judgments, and should *first of all* make an attempt to understand the difficulties, the actual problems, which surround the struggle of those in power. That would be a good exercise in keeping the commandment to honor the power.* It would be a matter of respecting it, not of suspecting it in everything it does. Hundreds of times in the past ten years we have heard Christian intellectuals remark: "*Any time* the mayor, or a member of the administration says it, it's false!" Is that honoring the power? (I am not saying, on the other hand, that we should say what has long been said: "*Any time* de Gaulle says it, it's true." I am not talking about an unconditional and irrational trust!) I simply observe that Christians believe the most unlikely charges, the most outrageous stupidities, and they treat as facts what are pure allegations backed up only by pretended proofs, as long as these are against the government.

It is striking that those intellectuals who are very exacting on the level of the problem-areas of philosophy, theological analysis or biblical criticism, show themselves quite lax when it comes to serious political judgment. It is not responsible to settle a question by saying: "One

* Romans 13:7; 1 Peter 2:17.

has only to . . . ," thus refusing to see the real difficulties and the probable consequences. That was the approach, for example, of 80% of our intellectuals toward the war in Algeria (those on the right as much as those on the left). It is not responsible to present a government with a moral imperative *under the pretense that it is workable,* when one is not himself burdened with the task of applying it. It is not responsible to pass motions and sign petitions which one would not be able to put into effect if one occupied the post of responsibility.

Let no one reply with a sweep of the hand: "Oh well . . . stop taking it seriously!" (that was said to me, in substance). That is exactly what being irresponsible is! All the statements according to which we bear the guilt for what is done in Algeria, etc. . . . , and even public fasts, all those things are mere words, because the critical attitude which I am denouncing is, in fact, a way of satisfying one's conscience.

Once again, let us repeat that in analyzing that attitude it is I, first of all, who am being probed, I as a member of the Church along with the others.

*   *   *

7

The Orientation of Christians

I would much prefer not to step out of all these nega-
tives. I would rather, from this point on, that each
Christian *discover* for himself, and in and for the
Church, the true thinking about politics, the desired approach. If I continue, if I write this final chapter against
my will, it is out of weakness, in order not to be accused
of never presenting anything but negative judgments,
criticisms and pessimism.

I. Let us be clear, once again, that all the preceding discussion ought not make a person give up his interest in
politics and adopt an apolitical attitude. I am not taking back anything of what I have written hundreds of
times:

(a) The Christian life is one. Therefore, in the
world in which we are living, it implies a certain participation in politics.

(b) Biblical teaching is definite on the value and place of politics, and on the absence of any separation between the spiritual and the temporal.

(c) The command to be present to the life of the world is likewise very definite.

But that is the prior condition for preaching the Gospel and receiving the faith. The participation in politics and the presence to the world have *no* value in themselves. It is not the vocation of the Church to promote a political or economic regime, or the welfare state, or socialism. Likewise it is not her business to advocate political solutions or to take sides in debates, which are generally exciting but superficial. The sole duty of the Church (in politics as well as in all else) is to take her stand in relation to the question: "When the Son of man comes, will he find faith on earth?"

As I see it, that involves three fundamental consequences, which I present in propositional form, without further development:

1. The Church's stance in politics (hence that of each Christian) should be specific and unique, not commensurate with the attitudes of the "pagans." The pagans can take care of their own affairs very well without outside help. The vocation of the Church is not to defend anticolonialism or colonialism, nor to promote superior techniques or industrialization, etc. (I reject as completely non-Christian the report of December 1956, of the ecumenical Council of Churches on the responsibility of Christians in the modern world.) But there is necessarily lacking in politics a dimension, a point of reference, an orientation, a value, in the absence of which politics remains halting and alienating. That fac-

tor no one is giving consideration to nor taking an interest in. It is exactly in that area that Christians have a specific and unique task. They have a function in politics, a vocation which is irreplaceable, but also incommunicable!

2. The Church's stance can only result from a future-now-in-process. It cannot result from an exegesis of the creation (with a legalistic picture, an order given at the beginning, and a causal view of succeeding events); nor from an eschatology which is purely ultimate, having no common measure with current happenings; nor from a lordship of Jesus Christ which is completed (with the course of the future seen as its continuation, and with an existential view of politics). It is a matter of the Lord in process of coming; that is, of a future which is drawing near. It is a matter of the Kingdom of God, radically different yet already present in secret, in mystery, in weakness, under the species of the Kingdom of Heaven. It is a matter of a coming judgment from which there is no escape, yet which is *embraced* in grace (not of a judgment in the past, over and done with, left behind and therefore of no importance, since grace has abounded all the more).

3. Finally, the Church is called to speak on the basis of revelation, not on the basis of the happenings and proddings of the world. We shall come back to that.

II. What we said in Chapter 4 (p. 123) could give the impression that we favor a policy of conformity to the State. That is not at all the case! I believe that the Church and Christians should stand in an attitude of permanent tension with respect to the world and the

State. To be in the world without belonging to the world implies a presence to all the world's activities and enterprises, but not a participation in them—just as the white horseman of the apocalypse rides with the others but takes no part in their individual works.

This presence implies, for one thing, a recognition of what the world is doing in line with its own principles, criteria and laws (it is not for us to offer it suggestions in the nature of methodological solutions or of moral judgments). It implies, for another thing, a rejection of the significance which the world attributes to its works, and *the attribution to them of an authentic significance.* This involves us in a tension, because it is obvious that the world and the State are going to reject the significance and implications which revelation ascribes to their history. In so doing, the Church and Christians fulfill a function on behalf of the world and the State which is entirely positive.

The tendency of the world and the State is, in fact, to become fulfilled and then to shut themselves up again in self-possession. The principal and decisive role (so seldom played by Christians) is precisely that of keeping situations open through this tension and challenge, and of preventing the termination and cloture of action. The radical *"No,"* which it is ours to pronounce over the course of the world and the activities of the State, is not a "negative" "No" of rupture. It is a "positive" "No" of *relationship.* It is not a question of pronouncing this "No" in order to consign the world and the State to darkness and hell, but in order to pronounce it *upon* their darkness as a proclamation of salvation.

We must get rid of the unfortunate illusion that the proclamation of salvation in the world implies acceding to the works of the world. The opposite is true! Yet we find ourselves in a situation, on the one hand, of constantly renewed dialogue, for it is quite obviously not a matter of total rejection, and, on the other hand, of a "No" *in abstracto* (which would be the negative "No")! We must not forget the first point, which is the presence to all the world's activities, while holding them at arm's length for the purpose of assigning them a different value than the value men claim for them when they pursue their politics, develop constitutions and economic administrations, initiate opinion trends and ideological movements and apply their techniques.

In the presence of the State, that involves, for one thing, a recognition of politics in its autonomy, and a tough, unvarnished realism toward political facts and methods, in full knowledge that the State cannot do otherwise and that politics presupposes hands which are really soiled! But once that is recognized and accepted as a fact of the political world, it implies in return the most radical affirmation of "no compromise," a limitation on all the powers of the State and a rejection of violence, all this within a declaration of the lordship of the State, but also within the declaration of the lordship of Jesus Christ. That means, for example, rendering honor to the State precisely because it is not worthy of that honor. It also means that under those circumstances it takes a Christian to honor the State.

Without this double affirmation there can be nothing but moral stands, the search for unsatisfactory agreements, compromises, false justifications and pretenses at purity. It is also in relation to this double affirmation that prayers for those in authority take on genuine meaning, in place of the politico-theological judgments which we encounter endlessly in all modern writing. This double affirmation expresses the tension in which the Christian should stand in relation to the world, and which he should force the world to experience.

This tension has nothing to do with party activities, industrialization, campaigns for peace, the welfare state or the crusade against hunger. It is much more weighty politically, much more decisive for the political future of the world. It is a tension which results both from the uncompromising nature of the Word of God, of which we are the bearers, and from the rejection on the part of the world of every truth of God. But that uncompromising quality and that rejection are not mutually exclusive, any more than the wrath of God causes the anger and revolt of the world to disappear just because it embraces them within itself. The tension is nothing other than the ethical and political disclosure of the "No" and the "Yes" pronounced by God in Jesus Christ over the lives of each one of us, over man's works and over the whole of our history.

In the concrete this tension is, in the end, what will enable political action to keep finding a springboard other than mere obedience to the force of circumstances. It is what will enable the history of mankind to unroll other than as a mere chain of economic or social principles. But the moment Christians and the Church relax this tension (which is what the world ardently wants, and which it obtains by domesticating the Church and interesting her in its works), then history reverts to a mechanical unfolding of events, and politics becomes a sad deception of fate.

III. To carry this out, the Church and Christians have to take as their starting point revelation, the Gospel, originality (in the etymological sense), the Word of God. The Church does not have to base herself on current events, nor be possessed by the news-output, nor react to everything that happens. She should base herself on that which makes her the Church, that is, on her election by God, and on the revelation committed to her as a precious deposit. That alone can be her point of departure. There she must constantly return to find her roots; which will mean that she has no need to find her place in relation to the happenings of the world, nor to modernize herself in order to belong to her age.

The reverse action is the true one. She should place the world in relation to herself. She should give meaning to events in terms of the revelation (and not try to slip the revelation into the gaps of the world's activities!). She should *bring about* the event instead of trailing it, submitting to it, or trying to explain it. Augustine, Bernard of Clairvaux, and Luther, for example, are men who brought about the event, and that is what the Church has been like whenever she has been faithful.

It is not the originality of knowledge, nor of situations, still less of the passion for politics, which is to spur the Church, but rather the originality of the Word of God. The important thing to make known, to let people see, to express by word and deed, is that the Word is truly the origin (the origin also of this remarkable and interesting current scene, etc.); that this Word is a fresh and surprising dimension of what is now happening; that this Word expresses the presence of the Wholly Other, and of that which measures everything going to make up the history of man.

It is in taking that origin that we shall perhaps have something to say and do in today's world. In other words, in place of the usual mode of approach (pondering the political events, becoming aware that they require us to say something, then racking our brains for what to say), we need resolutely to listen to the eternal Word of God, who perhaps will first give us something to think, then afterward something to say "in truth," which just might inject itself into the political scene.

That possibility is open to us because we are free in Christ, and because that liberty includes as well a freedom toward politics and toward current events. It is not because we might be more intelligent than others, nor because we may have a disinterested attitude toward politics, but because Christ is the Liberator. In him we are delivered from the pseudo-theater of current events and of political passion. We are not *in* politics. It is there *to get into,* to lend ourselves to, as a pure act of will, as an outright decision, with the freedom not to do so or to do so, with a will born of independent thinking, with the concern to do something special in it, instead of merging with the crowd, with "the people." And if the Word of God is silent today, then we too should be silent and repent.

IV. This very special task presupposes that the Church, in order to express herself and intervene, is seeking what is truly her own level, that which is within her

competence. We were saying how distressing it is to see
Christians make a particular show of their incompetence in political matters, and to act like people eager
for action. The Church, and Christians generally, have
clearly no competence in economic and political problems properly so called. That truly is not their place.
Whenever, for example, the Church attempts to insti-
tute a serious investigation into a current question, she
is caught unprepared and her conclusions arrive after
the event has been forgotten.

It seems to me that the Church and Christians should
concentrate on two categories of world problems. First,
those which are much more basic than current phenomena. There are in the world a certain number of
key points, or pivots, around which everything is ar-
ranged and functions. It is noteworthy that these are the
questions on which unanimity is evident. The Soviet
Union and the United States are in full accord, and a
Mendes-France government will behave just like a de
Gaulle government. The very fact of this unanimity
among enemy-brothers can be seen as proof that we are
dealing with a basic constituent of the modern world.

Now it would appear to me that it is precisely here
that it would be important for the Church to give expression to the revelation and to commit herself to an
active presence. For one thing, she would have time
to become completely informed, because these are
long-term phenomena. For another thing, it would involve continuous action on the Church's level (since its
implementation would be that of word and result, the
search for a life style).

Among these phenomena I shall cite: work, money,
technology, psychological effect, the emergence of new

religions (nationalism, communism), the nation-state,
etc. Compared with these phenomena, the things considered fundamental in journalistic opinion, such as anticolonialism or "the entrance into history of the third
world," are secondary, since the supposedly "new"
peoples merely place themselves on these foundations and enter into these journalistic molds. Let no
one say that these are phenomena which are well
known! I can reply, as one acquainted with the facts,
that they are as unknown as was the structure of the
atom two hundred years ago. There is need for a serious
theological study, which has not been done. There is
need for a serious sociological study, which is scarcely
outlined. It would be a matter of searching for a life
style, which is not even projected. To be sure, this is
much less thrilling than taking part in demonstrations
on the main boulevards!

2)   The other point at which, it seems to me, the Church
can intervene "on her own level," in the sphere of her
competence, is the vast domain of the psychic. The psychic has occupied an increasingly important place in
politics, in economics, and in the structure and life of
society. Social psychologists tell us, moreover, that modern man is living in a state of anguish, of anxiety and
fear, that he suffers from psychological loneliness, that
he is a prey to the rise of the irrational (which is a
source of suffering), to nebulous beliefs (and nationalism is no better than fortune-telling and astrology), etc.
I would think that here we are exactly at the point at
which the Church and Christians can act.

It could be at the political level, on the psychic and
emotional thread running through politics, to restore
the questions to their true place (and that is an action

which could have uncommon repercussions politically!).
Or it could also be at the level of the individual, in
the degree in which we have exactly the answer to the
evil from which the person in contemporary society
suffers. Yet we show very little concern for bringing it
to him! That would be a true presence of the Church to
the modern world, but it involves more activity of an
individual nature than of a group nature, more attention to the individual than to humanity. That is what
medical doctors, psychiatrists and urban workers are
discovering more and more. It would be a shame if the
Christians were the last to find it out.

V. In that role the Church could exercise a genuine
prophetic ministry. On the basis of a knowledge of the
profound social structures and of psychological reality,
she can in fact foresee (I am not, to be sure, confusing
prophecy with foresight!), for it is possible to foresee a
certain probable development of these structures and,
without any extraordinary competence, to point out the
consequences to be expected at a more superficial level.

But to put into operation that genuine prospective
(a much more responsible one than that which is currently being attempted) a great independence of judgment is indispensable. If, in fact, one remains bound to
the day-by-day happenings, if one becomes engrossed in
current events, if one gets involved in the uncertainties
of groups and political parties, if one believes that political competence is a matter of the weekly news output,
then by that very fact one becomes radically incapable
of all long-range political reflection. One becomes incapable even of the slightest foresight, for the reason that
foresight depends on reflection and knowledge and not

on the news. The obsession with news inhibits political thought, because news polarizes us around those political problems which are asserted massively, strikingly and publicly.

It seems to me that to the very extent that the Church depends upon another Lord and another Kingdom, for which she is ambassador to the world, she ought to have sufficient independence so that Christians would be capable of understanding the true issues with which man is to be faced tomorrow, in a manner very different from that of the partisan or the statistician. The giving of this warning would be extremely useful to mankind. It would be much more important than deciding in favor of a given solution, in a situation already at its climax or at the point of deterioration.

Now a mode of thinking sufficiently detached from the current superficialities, and concentrated on an analysis of the deeper movements, makes possible an actual forecast of the explosive happenings resulting from the latter. It was in 1930 that Christians should have alerted the world to decolonization, to Algeria and to Indochina. That is when the churches should have mobilized without letup. By 1956 those matters no longer held a shadow of interest. The socio-political process was already in operation, and it could not have made an iota of difference whether Christians got into the act or not. It would not have lessened a single atrocity nor resulted in a single act of justice. Likewise, it was in 1934 (the occupation of the Ruhr), or in 1935 (the war in Abyssinia), that Christians should have foretold the inevitable war against Nazism. That was when clarity of vision was essential. After 1937 it was too late. The fate of the world was already sealed for thirty years or more. But in those years the Christians, full of good intentions, were thinking only of peace and were loudly proclaiming pacifism! In matters of that kind, Christian good intentions are often disastrous.

Precisely because Christians should not be rooted in the current situations of the world, they (and they alone) ought to render the outstanding service of giving warning of political issues to come, which are going to be knotty and are threatening to appear. That would be an absolutely decisive service, because it would come at a time when political situations could still be resolved. That is the time when it is still possible to bring a just solution to bear, when human tragedy might still be averted. That is also the time when the mechanisms of a given line of development are not yet in place, when a person can, as a person, intervene with his freedom. Once the mechanisms are assembled and put together there can only be a sequence of fatalities against which a person is helpless.

I am saying that Christians *alone* are capable of carrying out that mission, since they are the only ones in a position to call in question the current situations freely and decisively, because they are not "of the world." When they fail to do so they are gravely at fault. That is their political sin *par excellence,* a sin which proves that they are "of the world," whether because they are stuck fast in their personal situations (position, money, family, ecclesiastical tradition), or whether, like larks, they are hypnotized by the mirror of the politics of the moment. It amounts to the same thing!

I am saying that this forewarning is part of the duty of a Christian in the body politic. It is exactly the function of the watchman often spoken of in scripture. He has constantly to alert man on behalf of God, not only of the great acts of God in history, but also of the trend of that history. This implies a judgment on that trend, and not an attitude of hands-off based on the notion that the course of history is justified in itself.

Let us not object that this presupposes an extraordinary clairvoyance and an exceptional political competence. The function should be assumed in and by the Church, so that it would be carried out with an interchange of knowledge and judgment. But more than that, the thing which prevents us from seeing and grasping probable developments is the fact that, anchored in our positions, wound up in our activities and confident that things should take a turn for the better, we obstinately refuse to consider the trend of events. It is that refusal that the faith in Jesus Christ should rid us of, and just that riddance removes the blindfold from our eyes. Finally, in this role of foresight, the light shed upon the world by the Holy Spirit, and seen by faith, has a part.

All this shows the possibility for prediction available to the Christian, and his guilt toward mankind if he fails to make use of it. "If . . . you give him no warning . . . his blood shall I require at your hand." * To be sure, this forewarning is not prophecy, but it is not unrelated to it. If there have been no more prophets, in the Old Testament sense, since John the Baptist, if in the New Testament passages the prophets have an altogether different charisma, there is still the matter of proclaiming the lordship of Jesus Christ in a given historic situation, in a world which is characteristic and well defined. It is

* Ezekiel 3:18.

not a question of abstract, generalized and metaphysical preaching.

So the forewarning is not the announcement of an extraordinary act of God in the world, but rather the point at which the proclamation of the lordship of Jesus Christ can call man to change not only his life but the history of his society, thanks to the grace and the love of God revealed in Jesus Christ. Finally, it is a new expression of the situation of tension which we outlined above.

VI. *The ministry of reconciliation.* Everyone readily agrees with the principle that the Church and Christians have a ministry of reconciliation to perform in the world. We know that Christians go into politics with that in mind, and that is not false; but we generally do not sufficiently reflect on the conditions which are implied by the exercise of that ministry.

(a) We often hear Christians who are active in a political party say that they are doing so in obedience to that vocation. Well and good! But the true reconciliation is that which, in consequence of the reconciliation of God with man effected in Jesus Christ, unites Christians among themselves. The model for what the ultimate reconciliation is to be is given there, and only there. Every reconciliation to which we try to give expression among men can be derived only from that one. Hence we absolutely cannot claim to be exercising that ministry on the outside while destroying, or threatening to destroy, the reconciliation of and in the Church.

This means, first of all, that whenever we join a party we should always be spiritually and humanly *closer, more bound, more friendly, more trusting and more open* with respect to our brothers in the Church, even if they be sometimes of a different opinion politically, than we are with respect to our fellow party-members. Reconciliation does not mean reuniting with those who have the same opinions we have. It means loving and bearing with those who are opposed. Now that can only be done first in the Church.

It is good that there should be Christians active in the various parties, even the communist party or the OAS if need be, since that can be an occasion for demonstrating to the world that faith in the same Saviour infinitely transcends those differences, and that Christians of opposite parties, or of enemy nations, are *first and foremost* brothers in Christ and completely understand one another spiritually and humanly. If such is not the case, then involvement in a party has nothing to do with the ministry of reconciliation. You cannot pretend to reconcile others if you are not reconciled among yourselves.

That assumes, for example, that we will not take part in peremptory quarrels, nor pass judgment on our brothers, nor resent the opposing opinion of a brother. It also assumes that within the party we shall never cease to affirm the independence the faith establishes, *by witnessing to our ties* with our brothers in the faith, even though they be our political opponents. There again we encounter tension, but that is the price of a reconciliation which really means something. Otherwise it is merely another word for a nice humanistic agreement.

It also presupposes that a pastor cannot involve himself in a party, nor make a public issue out of outright political positions. That is a bondage of the ministry. For if the pastor is supposed to be the "leader of the flock," he should not be injecting division. He should avoid being a stumbling block to the weak, to the nonpolitical, etc. He ought not to scatter the sheep, which is necessarily what would happen were he to take strict political stands. Surrounded by the various and multiple commitments of the faithful, he should be the one who remains impartial, outside of party, ready to hear all, to understand all, to have the confidence of all (which he no longer has once he becomes partisan); ready also to reconcile Christians of opposite leanings.

That path of mutual understanding, of love over and above conflicting decisions, has to be followed at the cost of a great deal of effort. It is not at all natural. It is not to be taken for granted (that is all too evident!). There has to be someone in the Church to urge each of us in that direction. Someone has to be the guide and counselor accepted by all. Only the pastor can do that.

But there can only be understanding and harmony among the faithful on condition that the pastor not belong to one of the coteries. It is not a matter of his being an umpire. It is much more than that. He must be the image of the Reconciler himself. If a pastor rejects this bondage, it means that he places political commitment above doing the truth in love. From that time on, he must realize that he is no longer exercising the pastoral ministry.

(b) In the second place, reconciliation implies that one of the great functions of Christians in the political world is to calm down debate, and this not only within the Church but especially outside. Most political problems today are dreadfully distorted by passion and by the excesses of public opinion. Very often, questions which are relatively simple are made insoluble by concerned groups which are overwrought and resentful, with the result that the most normal solutions become unacceptable. A victory of one side over the other is the only remaining possibility, which means a triumph of intolerance in the end, and more often than not the imposition of an injustice.

The first task of reconciliation for Christians would be to help opposite sides to understand each other, to defuse the explosive issues, to calm passions, in order to lead each side back to a reasonable view of things. That, obviously, is a far less easy task than that of fanning the flames. It is also far less thrilling for youth. It presupposes, for example, that one seek to reduce the size of the stakes, and also the opinion gap between the two sides, to minimize the very weight of the question at issue. The Christian ought never entertain exaggerated statements (for example: "All France is at stake in the Algerian War," or "We must destroy the OAS by all the means available," etc.).

Now I am obliged to observe that Christians intervene in political debates mostly in order to point up positions by bringing theological justifications to bear. In so doing, they throw oil on the fire. The vocation of calming down debate strictly forbids, in particular, the appeal to public opinion. Every time a petition is circulated, a poster is put up or a public meeting is called, it never fails to excite the crowd, to inflame public opinion and to raise a mob against something. That does not lead to reasonable attitudes but to attitudes of passion.

It never points toward the solution of a problem, but toward the outbreak of a conflict and to the generation of hatred and mutual accusation. The intervention of an aroused public opinion hardens all the factional tendencies (including those one is fighting against), makes positions irreversible and adversaries irreconcilable.

The appeal to public opinion looks like a good tactic. As a matter of fact, it always results in the frightful entangling of political situations, for when public opinion is aroused by means which are nothing more than propaganda it is no longer capable of rendering political judgment. All it can do is to follow the leaders. That the stirring up of public opinion should be a method employed by those who see the struggle of interests and classes not only as a fact but as a thing to be desired, as something favorable, as an instrument of war, is normal; but for those who are exercising on earth the ministry of reconciliation it is inadmissible. A Christian aware of that vocation can never appeal to public opinion except to sober it, to dissuade it, to calm it down. The emotion of the crowd is never an instrument of God's justice, for it is always of the order of wrath and can only add injustice to injustice.

I am aware that this will be criticized as a defense of the status quo. That is definitely not true. Christians have indeed to lay these situations on the line, but by other methods. The effort toward reconciliation in the struggle of interests, opinions, nations or classes (which is a fact) can neither be used for social conservatism nor for prolonging the alienation. It is a question of finding other forms of liberation and another mode of entry for Christians. That is where we should apply *all* the thought, all the charity, all the creativity, all the insight of which Christians are capable.

Whenever there is political action on the part of the Church, that action should be as discreet as possible. If the Church thinks it good to intervene in a given situation, in support of a certain solution, that should take the form of a personal dialogue with the authority. Too often, alas, the Church is asked to speak out loud in order to draw attention to herself. Now a political action should never be carried out for the sake of being seen, of showing oneself off to the world! If that is done one falls precisely into the attitude condemned by Jesus (Matt. 23:5). The pharisees were virtuous in order to be seen of men. Virtue today consists of social and political action. To ask the Church to act publicly in order to be in line with public opinion is to emulate the pharisees.

Everything should be open and aboveboard, certainly. There should be no secret diplomacy, but no methods of publicity and agitation either. These things are even more serious in our day than secrecy. Every time one seeks to "arouse public opinion" it means that one has disavowed the ministry of reconciliation.

(c) The reconciliation of which we have just been speaking has to do especially with the general attitude in society as a whole. But with that should go along a certain attitude, a certain action within the group in which we are involved, whether it be a union, or a political party, or a commercial or industrial enterprise, or a university, or a sports club. We belong to groups which are in opposition, in competition and in conflict with others, so we have this function of reconciliation to fulfill within our group with respect to the others. That leads to certain inferences.

It presupposes, for example, that within our group we should try to introduce a degree of moderation with regard to the "cause" or the "concerns." We are not going to act like "true believers," absolutizing the doctrines of our party or of our business. On the contrary, we shall try *within our group* to be interpreters for others. Just as at the personal level we have to take into account the interests of others, so likewise we should try to give those in our own group an insight into the point of view of others. Why does that fellow act differently from me? That is what we have to explain if we are to bring the conflicts back to a modicum of humanity. Thus it will not be a matter of reinforcing our party positions, of supplying new arguments and new ways to win. It will rather be a matter of humanizing situations, of playing the role of advocates for the opposition, of being interpreters for all.

Obviously, that will make us the butt of some harsh criticism. We will be called saboteurs, traitors, fifth columnists! But if we have enough humility, charity and devotion within the group, it is also possible to survive those accusations. If we win people's confidence sufficiently, we might in fact get to the point of being representatives of those whose ideas and situations we do not share, so that in effect a true dialogue might take place. This would not be the false, power-to-power dialogue constantly taking place in the world, which is never anything but a test of strength, with one side ultimately predominating. It would be, to the contrary, a dialogue within each group through the medium of Christians in each of the opposing groups, who are deeply united

[margin handwritten note:] emph on reconciliation

among themselves because they are first of all in the Church. They would be in a position to gain a hearing for the reasons and interests of the other side, with those members of their respective groups whose confidence they had gained.

That would prohibit our transforming political positions into issues of finality and arriving at definitive judgments on current situations. It obviously implies that, if I am in more or less agreement with the ideas and decisions of my own group, whether by deliberate choice or for purely sociological reasons, I cannot take them with total seriousness. For me, it cannot be a matter of the commitment of my total self. Socialism, capitalism, scientific development, national independence, etc., etc., are issues not without value or importance, but they certainly are not worth the death of a human being, and that is true in the very degree to which they are ideologies and global images. But, in the various groups, real factors are transformed in this manner into ideologies.

Finally, in our respective groups we have to give attention to the means employed for expressing our ideas and interests. It is, in the last analysis, through those means—posters, speeches, leaflets, etc.—that we reach people. We should make known our objections of conscience against methods of aggressiveness which appeal to hate and contempt, and which pass summary and inaccurate judgments; or again, against methods of bribery and blackmail, against the use of pressure by powerful interests, etc. That also constitutes part of our ministry of reconciliation.

For we have to face up in the end. To be reconciled is well and good, but with whom, if not with the person who is our enemy? The man of the right has no problem being reconciled with the army, nor the man of the left with the FLN. The capitalist has no trouble reconciling himself with the bourgeoisie, nor the union leader with the working man, but that is not reconciliation! If one is to have a realistic picture of this reconciliation, he will come to grips with the great difficulty to be encountered, with the extent to which reconciliation presupposes not only faith but personal qualities as well, such as self-discipline and self-criticism.

We are presented with a genuine ministry which cannot be entrusted to everybody (such as the very weak), and which cannot be made to depend on the individual commitments of the moment. A genuine Church life would take it for granted that decisions of that magnitude would be made in conjunction with the investigation, the prayer and the need of the religious community.

VII. Together with this ministry of reconciliation in the midst of the world, witnessing to and referring back to the work of reconciliation wrought by God himself in Jesus Christ, the Church should lend her aid to the world along the road on which it is traveling (this road is also that of the Church, to the extent to which she is a sociological body, and also in view of the fact that she is a special body submerged in the world, like the treasure in the field, the salt in the food, and the leaven in the dough, intermingled yet distinct, incorporated yet different). She is not the world's servant, never! She should never become lost in the world! She is not there to help society or man to succeed in their own projects in accordance with their own intentions (which are always an expression of the revolt against God and, in the last analysis, of sin in one form or another). Yet she cannot claim to be naturally apart, as we indicated above. Like it or not, she is in the world, and the world enters into her.

Henceforth she should have her part to play in relation to the world's works, to society and to man. It is not her function to suggest theories or, as we said above, solutions. It is not for her to lay before the world a doctrine of man and of the State. The theology of man and of the State is for the internal use of the Church. If she puts these out to society at large, they will become just one more theory, neatly ticketed and put away in the idealist's wardrobe. But in terms of that theology, expressing revelation *hic et nunc,* she should provide society and man with reference points and sighting points. She should lay down certain requirements.

Once again, in all these "services" we find a "tension." There are points of reference which can, for example, make it possible for man to find a meaning in what he does, but which could also orient him concerning the real direction in which his undertakings are headed. Man thinks he is going in a certain direction, which he has determined on the basis of his knowledge and ambitions. It is essential to remind him that each one of his works is polyvalent, that it is subject to different levels of interpretation, that he will hit different targets than those he was aiming at, etc. Thus the Church should attempt to enlighten man and society on what they are doing and undertaking, not in order to dissuade them, but in order to make things clear, to see

to it that the stakes are in full view and that the rules of
the game are honest, that there be no self-justification,
either in the undertaking or in the results.

The Church can also furnish man and society with
sighting points. These are not, strictly speaking, values;
but she can restore the world's values to their true place
before God, and she can reveal to man the true direction. In this way the Church today can perfectly well
foster democracy, or secularity, but by expressing their
profound truth. For example, she should make it plain
that democracy is neither a just regime nor a legitimate
one (the absurdity of the sovereignty of the people,
etc.), an efficient regime nor, still less, a Christian one;
but rather that it is the weakest, the most humble, the
most open of regimes; that it is the least dangerous, the
least efficient, the least oppressive of regimes; that hence
it is impossible to acknowledge a democracy fitted out
in armor and high productivity and equipped with
plans and insurance policies, and that a choice has to be
made between democracy and efficiency.
The same is true of secularity. There must be firm insistence that the State does not decide truth, nor incarnate religious ideology. It is not the business of the
State to choose a philosophy, since there is no human
truth, still less governmental truth. In view of this,
there must be a radical rejection of the Hitlerian State
as well as of the communist State and of Franco's State,
which are not secular States. It goes without saying that
for that reason the Church cannot ask the support of
the State. And since the State must not formulate the
truth about anything, it is necessarily limited; it cannot
become an absolute, either in itself or in its works.

Similarly the Church in our day can, for example, undertake the defense of "reason" against the frenzies, the passions, the rise of the forces of darkness, against modern religions and the *hubris* (pride) which characterize this society. She should call natural man to a reasonable behavior and judgment, not because reason has a value in and of itself, nor because it would open the doors of truth to man, but because it brings man back to his true level, because (unless it gives birth to rationalism!) it closes the religious, the spiritual and the mystical escape routes, and in the end drives man into a corner.

These examples, and I could give others, show what I mean when I speak of sighting points. They are points which the world itself has *chosen,* but to which the Church should assign a true place and a true significance. In other words, the Church should listen very carefully to what men and the world are saying. She ought not reject it as devoid of value. But on the one hand she should enlighten the speaker concerning the real meaning of what he is saying, and on the other hand she should, in a certain sense, declare herself the uncompromising guardian of that which man has chosen, of the rules of the game he has devised. "You say 'justice,' 'freedom.' All right. Justice: this . . . Freedom: that . . . And now let's get down to business. Let's remember together what you have just said. Let's consider that no justice is done through a lot of injustices, and that freedom owes nothing to dictatorship, etc."

In other words, the Church again (because she is the people of the God who speaks, whose Son is the Word, and whose Word is creative and redemptive) should take man's words seriously, more seriously than does the

very man who speaks them. She should invest these
words with their full significance and should remind
man of the sense of his words. She should require of
man that he hold to his word, and this on all levels . . .
from the most elementary (the word given, the commitment entered into—and in view of this the Church cannot go along with a kind of existentialism of the discon-
tinuity of the person, and of the fluctuation of words
according to circumstances) to the most exalted (the
word which assigns to a people the values of its being
and the meaning of its history).

Finally, in carrying out this work the Church states
some requirements. These are not moral requirements
(to obey a law, a humanism), or spiritual requirements
(to give official recognition to the true God). They are
requirements which, in accordance with the reference
points and the sighting points, implement a continual
calling-in-question *from inside a given society,* a constant clarifying, a stocktaking of what one is about, an
urge toward renewal which, in the final analysis, is
revolutionary with respect to *every* form of society or
State.* If the Church were truly this permanent dissatis-
faction at the heart of societies, which she ought to be,
she would play a dynamic role, instead of being forever
in the funeral procession of the past.

VIII. But, in the very degree to which the Church and
Christians are witnesses to the one true God who has re-

---

* And therefore, with respect to a State which calls itself revolutionary,
the Church will necessarily be accused of being counterrevolutionary,
not because she wants to step back and defend outworn positions, as is
often the case, but because she demands that the State go beyond the
stage in which it tends inevitably to become bogged down.

vealed himself, they have the stern duty of desacralization and demystification to perform in society. After the
"Yes," of which we gave some examples in the previous
section, there comes the "No." But it is not a "No" on
the works themselves, on their reality or their value. It
is not an intrinsic judgment (which the Church is incapable of passing) nor a final, last judgment (which the
Church has not the right to pronounce). It is, in fact, a
"No" on the religion which man constructs on the basis
of his works.

It is directed toward man's sacralizing—his calling sacred—his own works, the myth he builds up, not in
order to face his destiny and to try to find the key to his
life, but in order to magnify himself in his works. Because we are witnesses to the true God, we have to reject
such sacralizing, just as the first Christians rejected the
calling sacred of nature, and the Reformation likewise
rejected the sacred progressively restored in the Middle
Ages. We have that operation to resume in the present
age.

Man is not content to build a world. He has to endow
it with an ultimate value and himself insert it into the
category of the sacred. But the sacred today is no longer
that of nature. It is the sacred of man's own works. We
can very well accept the works of man in their humility,
their relativity, their materiality, but we must rigorously destroy all claim to the religious or the sacred. We
must profane by our *conduct*, not by statements or
theories, the sacred of money, the sacred of the State
(which means that the State and politics are reduced to
their function of managing the material interests of a
collectivity, an honorable function but not one involving any excessive valuing or sacralizing, all this in ac-

cordance with the doctrine of the secularity of the
State), the sacred of the Nation (which means that we
can very well accept the sociological structure of the
nation as a framework like any other and variable according to historic circumstances, but that it is inadmissible to support a nationalism, the glorification of a
national sacred, with all the vocabulary that goes with it
—the Eternal Nation, the Historically Necessary Nation, the Value Nation, etc., etc.).

All should be ruthlessly destroyed. Likewise, even
though we can't press it too far, we have to reject the sacred of work, of technology, of science, of production. It
is, above all else, a matter of spiritual combat. The presence to the world should take place on the level of the
world's adorations, and its procedure should be like
that described, for example, in Jeremiah 5:19.

Once again, if we were to perform this work it would
not be negative. It would not be against man. We know
very well that man has always been able to do better
whenever he has been freed from the sacred which he
set up for himself, and which held him prisoner. The
very fact of reducing man's work, and man himself, to
the most naked reality is an entirely positive operation,
an act of humility. It is a "presence to the world" far
more genuine and important than all the traditional
participations and justifications.

The same is true concerning myths. We have already
said that it is important that modern thought should
have discovered this mythical dimension in which man
lives. Myth is not a form of expression belonging to the
past. Our contemporary society is a great creator of
myths and rests upon myths. At a time when much is

being said about demythologizing (in religious vocabulary), we observe a prodigious flowering of myths. But it is worth noting that the demythologizing enterprise is concentrated on the myths of yesterday and the day before, never on those of today. The left, which claims to take the lead in the undertaking, is itself ensnared in myths it doesn't see, or which it has created; the mythologizing of socialism, for example, as well as of progress or of history.

But, in truth, this seems to us unavoidable. One cannot, at the human level, combat a myth except thanks to another myth (Sorel saw that clearly, merely by extending Marx's concept of ideology). One can only destroy the myth of liberalism by the myth of socialism. For if, from one point of view, it can be said that myth gives us our thoughts, it is still more correct to say that myth supplies the only obligating and satisfying reasons for action. But that means that there never is any actual demythologizing. The man of the left today is a mythologized man, exactly as were the bourgeoisie *and* the proletariat in the nineteenth century, and sometimes the myths are the same (for example, those of work and of progress). Thus one has, in fact, brought man out of one alienation into another.

That is the process we are witnessing today with the global mutation of our societies. From alienation through the exploitation of man by man, we are passing into alienation through the incorporation of man into the Nation-State. In the one case as in the other, myth is the agent of total alienation, since it is that which makes it possible for man to accept the situation by interpreting it as entirely different from what it really is.

Only the liberation of man through the truth can both show him the real situation in which he finds himself, and at the same time release him from the myths which mystify and deceive him. But the truth can only play this role if it is not intrinsic to history, if it is not history. History is not liberation. It has no being independent of events, and events do not have liberating significance. The truth cannot be liberating unless it be the Wholly Other.

The truth which is Christ is truly liberating for man because it comes *from elsewhere,* but it *comes* into *this* human situation. Christ is not only the liberator for the person who has received the faith, but the person who has received the faith knows that this Christ is the liberator of every man (by promise and hope). That liberty in Christ is the only disalienation possible, and the only demystification.

That is why it seems amazing to me that in the Church we should get lost in these crossroads and blind alleys, which consist in applying the myth theory to scripture, and in trying to demythologize scripture on the basis of purely human ideas about myth, when what needs to be done is just the reverse. Scripture itself was the most destructive acid with respect to myths. It is the revelation contained in the Bible (and there alone) which can demythologize man's current situation, a situation continually in flux. Here lies the task and not in demythologizing scripture, which makes little sense and is impossible besides!

How can we fail to realize that scripture, *in precisely the same way in which the myths contained in scripture itself are treated,* is the true destroyer of myths? How can we fail to see that one need only apply this to politics, to nationalism, to communism, to science, etc., in order to reduce them all to changeable undertakings which are meaningless in themselves? Precisely as the Church *should* have done formerly with respect to capitalism, the bourgeois morality, and money. But all that is just about dead, and no longer concerns us.

To destroy the myths is to disalienate man, but it is also, in many cases, to rob him of his reasons for acting, his hopes. While it is socially and politically indispensable to bring man back to reality, it can also commit him to despair. Hopes may be false and ideologies absurd, yet they are still the source of action and life. Therefore it would be a cruel act to destroy them without more ado. So here again I see the peculiar and unique task of Christians. Insofar as it is the truth which brings man back to the real, insofar as it is that hope which doesn't deceive that destroys the deluded judgments, to that extent there is no room for despair. Thus the proclamation of the hope and the love which are in Christ goes unfailingly along with demystification and desacralization. The latter cannot really be carried out except in company with this witness and this charity.

But we must not conclude, as do some theologians, that one need only preach the Word in order to have the myths, the idols and the false hopes collapse. That does not follow. It is absolutely not to be taken for granted. The preaching of the Word also involves open combat against idols, and the prophets constantly set the example for this. Once again, the two aspects, the "No" and the "Yes," have to be set forth and affirmed. If the presence of the true God entails of itself the collapse of the false, the proclamation of the Gospel implies, for the liberation of the person to whom it is proclaimed, the indictment of that which holds him captive.

IX. *Opening up the world.* The world, ever since it has been the world, seeks to close itself up, to shut itself in, to exclude God, to make itself one and complete. Society wants to be "integrated," that is, to bring about the complete integration of all its component parts, and the assimilation and complete conformity of all its people. The State wants to be all, that is, to embrace all the activities of the group, to control everything, to blueprint everything, to make provision for everything, to leave no room for the unpredictable which is man's freedom, and still less for that supreme unpredictable which is the intervention of God. Again, that is what the Old Testament describes for us with Enoch, Babel, Ecclesiastes and Ezekiel.

It is the same endeavor we are witnessing today, except that we are possessed of more powerful means, and we cover the entire planet. It is the establishing of a total world. We should realize that its will to assimilate the person (which could not be done except on the basis of economic activity and increased consumption, possible only in and through the group) is identical with its will to exclude God. And it is the scandal and the appalling heresy of Teilhard de Chardin to pretend to bless this totalism of the world in the name of Christianity; but that cannot be done, as is evident from his writings, without leaving to one side the incarnation of Christ in the person of Jesus, that is, by ultimately depersonalizing God, and by turning Christ into a point, into a complete geometric abstraction.

Now the Old Testament shows us that God, faced with man's claim to set up a closed world for himself, continually reopens the breach. The Church should always be the breach in an enclosed world: in the world of Sartre's private individual as well as in the worlds of the perfection of technology, the totalism of politics or the strongbox of the kingdom of money. It all amounts to the same thing. Christians have their role to play, which might seem deceptive and harmful, of preventing the world from attaining its own perfection along one or the other of its paths (I am not saying *perfection*, which would mean the Kingdom of God, but *its* perfection, in the sense of *"Die Perfektion der Technik,"* for example).

Thus the Church should preserve the openness *of* the world (just the reverse of the attitude often recommended, that the Church should open herself *to* the world!!!). Our society, our State, should remain an open world, a world of possibilities and not a world in which everything is calculated ahead of time and provided for in advance, and in the last analysis made subject to necessity. It matters little that this necessity is the fruit of our own efforts. It is still necessity!

This openness of the world can be maintained first and foremost by preaching, but it must be strict and faithful preaching, not a preaching tailored to demands and to current interests (which blends with the world and serves to close it in on itself a little more!). It requires a preaching which is the event and the intervention of the Wholly Other and which, in consequence, is inevitably strange, not adapted to the world's aberrations; a preaching that is surprising and not in accord with the world's habits; disturbing and not reassuring. As the body of Christ (a body singularly foreign in relation to our society!), that is all the Church has to do. That is her sole charge and her sole function.

As far as Christians are concerned, they too have their essential role to play in maintaining the openness of the world. As a matter of fact, that is what we were describing above when we were speaking of participation in activities without participating in beliefs, ideologies, myths and expectations. All I was trying to show in the first six chapters was that, precisely in our own day, Christians are completely imbued with these beliefs, ideologies, myths and expectations, and the cleanup job seems to me to have the priority, to be the most urgent task facing the Church. If this participation in illusory ideologies is the price Christians have to pay in order to "live in the world," then they had better stay in their own ghetto! It will amount to the same thing in the end for the world. One can only hope that some personal faith will survive and some individual virtue will be practiced!

So it is up to Christians to relativize social, political and economic activities, by the use of a sense of humor, for example. They should avoid the language of exaggeration, of melodrama, of excessive indignation, approaches found so frequently in all the political articles by Christians. Rather it is a matter, in great friendliness toward the people who are implicated in these activities, of helping them understand that the life is worth more than food and the body than clothing, and that in the end all political, economic or social forms, all institutions, all patriotic activity, all resistance movements, all conquests, all liberations, all sociological structures and all businesses are mere clothing. In the last analysis they never attain to life.

I have few illusions. In spite of all precautions, I know very well that the first six chapters will be used by devotees of the spiritual as a pretext for the cleavage between faith and life. I know very well that those same chapters will be condemned by others as apolitical and pessimistic. I am fully aware that the proposals in the final chapter will be looked upon as ineffective and academic by those hungry for action, as superfluous by others and as impractical by all.

I know that—and yet I am determined to write, wondering within myself whether, in this present night in which Christians assuredly are not fulfilling their role as the light of the world, God may not eventually make use of one or the other of these lines to strike a tiny spark.